BURST THE BUBBLE

SUNG K. KWON

Pacific Press®
Publishing Association
Nampa, Idaho | Oshawa, Ontario, Canada
www.pacificpress.com

Cover design by Gerald Lee Monks
Cover design resources from istockphoto.com/Ann_Mei
Inside design by Aaron Troia

Additional copies of this book are available by calling toll-free 1-800-765-6955 or by visiting http://www.adventistbookcenter.com.

Library of Congress Cataloging-in-Publication Data
Names: Kwon, Sung Kun, author.
Title: Burst the bubble : finding your passion for community outreach / Sung K. Kwon.
Description: Nampa : Pacific Press Publishing Association, 2017.
Identifiers: LCCN 2017047696 | ISBN 9780816363414 (pbk.)
Subjects: LCSH: Mission of the church. | Church work. | Communities—Religious
    aspects—Christianity. | Evangelistic work. | Missions. | Missional church movement. |
    Seventh-day Adventists—Doctrines.
Classification: LCC BV601.8 .K86 2017 | DDC 253—dc23 LC record available at
    https://lccn.loc.gov/2017047696

November 2017

Contents

Preface

Ask yourself, "If my church were to close its doors, would anyone in the community notice, or would anyone in the community care?" Church is where disciples are equipped, developed, educated, and sent out to the local neighborhoods; church is to make a difference in an individual's life and its immediate communities. So why are we asking the above questions?

Perhaps we have forgotten our chosen status, just as the Israelites forgot their chosen status. We have forgotten about being a recognizable, tangible, and visible sign—a witness and foretaste of God's dream for the world. *Why are we here? What are we here to do?* Maybe we don't know what to do with this current life, but we desire to go to heaven and live forever.

Perhaps we've become systematic and mechanical religious practitioners. We come to church routinely, mechanically, and practice religion. But the church cannot be confined and limited to just a worship program; the church cannot be contained by its walls. A church is not just a place and time, where we meet for a weekly appointment. In addition, the church is not about just keeping the traditions and maintaining the status quo. In fact, we must plant our feet into the tradition and grow out of it. If we don't grow out of our own traditions, we will be ineffective and inefficient.

The church must be a missional movement; every Adventist church, educational institution, and hospital network must be missional. Archbishop of Canterbury Rowan Williams said, "It is not the church of God that has a mission. It's the God of mission that has a church."[1]

Therefore, the church is to be God's hands and feet in accomplishing God's mission. We need to equip and develop our church members into becoming effective workers with God.

Darrell Guder wrote,

> We ring our bells, conduct our worship services . . . , and wait for this very different world to come to us. We mount pulpits and preach sermons as we have done for centuries, before this new culture emerged. We pursue our internal arguments about doctrine and order as though nothing outside had changed. In effect, we continue to speak church Latin, expecting our immediate mission field, our world, to learn it and respond in our language.
>
> But much has changed.[2]

Perhaps we should stop asking ourselves, "What can we do to bring people into our church?" Instead we should ask, "What is God up to in this neighborhood?" and "What are the ways we need to change in order to engage the people in our community who no longer consider church a part of their lives?" This is why Ellen Whites summarized Christ's method as a lifetime commitment to the investment of the community—because it is a relationship, and we must establish a faithful presence until the second coming of Christ. Christianity is a progression; it is about connecting the church with the community through life-on-life evangelism.

Therefore, we must be incarnational and contextual in our community outreach ministries. We must listen to what people in our communities are pleading for. In fact, in my humble opinion, if pastors do not live in the community where their church is located, pastors don't have ministry; they have management. In addition, if church members do not live in their church community, they are not difference-makers—being salt and light of the community; they are churchgoers.

Unfortunately, some of us are so eager to tell others about our own brand of religion and to convince them that we are right and they are wrong, that we don't listen to what our neighbors are saying, and we can't see what they are experiencing.

Read this well-known parable of the prodigal son in Luke 15:13–16: "Not long after that, the younger son got together all he had, set off for a distant country and there squandered his wealth in wild living. After he had spent everything, there was a severe famine in that whole country, and he began to be in need. . . . He longed to fill his stomach with the pods that the pigs were eating, but no one gave him anything."

When we read and study the parable, we often focus on the younger son's irresponsibility and how he wasted his inheritance. However, if we look through the context-specific perspective of Russian pastors, they might say that it was a circumstantial challenge rather than an individual problem. There was "a severe famine in that whole country"—so, they question, Where was the government's support in this situation? Due to being a socialistic society, they will expect the government to take care of *all* the survivors from the disaster, including the younger son. For them, this story is not about personal responsibility.

Moreover, through the eyes of Tanzanian pastors, they may say the story is a serious dereliction of duty on the community's part, because "no one gave him anything." How come the community didn't give him anything to eat? As a collective society, Tanzanians take care of one another. If there is a neighbor in distress among them, they will care for them, visit them, provide and minister to their needs. Something is wrong with the community around the prodigal son. Therefore, Tanzanian pastors might also say the story is not about personal responsibility.

But most people will say it is about personal responsibility, because the younger son squandered the money he inherited. But, perhaps everyone is right, when the story is experienced through his or her own perspective and viewpoints of life.

Instead of connecting people to God through evangelism and worship, connecting people through community and discipleship, connecting people to the city through mercy and justice, and connecting people to the culture through the integration of faith and work, sometimes the church wants to be in control and dominate the religious agenda, policies, or operational procedures . . . just like the Pharisees. Where is our compassion to end poverty? Where is our vision to stop world hunger? Where is our dream to stop human trafficking? Where is our desire to build a happy home? Where is our commitment for a life of integrity and humility and peace? We are evangelists and disciples who love making disciples.

If we are not growing, equipping, developing, educating, and enlightening our church members to be a light to their family, neighborhood, community, society, the world, then what are we doing? Why do we exist? We should not be striving for material possessions and social status. We should not crave only financial success, external beauty, or career advancements. Daniel Joseph and Toby McKeehan said, "The greatest single cause of atheism in the world today is Christians who acknowledge Jesus with their lips then walk out the door and deny Him by their lifestyle. That is what an unbelieving world simply finds unbelievable."[3]

Every Adventist must be a faithful servant of God, for His mission. We must reach out to everyone—sharing, caring, and proclaiming the good news of God's redemptive work, so that people can see us as a recognizable, tangible, and visible sign of the kingdom of God on earth. It is not about being the best church *in* the community; it is about being the best church *for* the community.

"Alan Krieder observes that early Christianity grew explosively—40 percent per decade for nearly three centuries—in a very hostile environment," writes Timothy Keller.[4] Kreider said, "People were fascinated by it [Christianity], drawn to it as to a magnet."[5] Keller says Kreider "goes on to make a strong historical case that Christians' *lives*—their concern for the weak and the poor, their integrity in the face of persecution, their economic sharing, their sacrificial love even for their enemies, and the high quality of their common life together—attracted nonbelievers to the gospel."[6]

People must hear, see, touch, and feel Christianity. We must stop blowing hot air, and instead of focusing on doing events, we must focus on being the church. When we are externally focused, our objectives change—we will begin to focus on purpose, core values, visions, missions, partnerships with communities, evangelism through a long-term sustainable community development, creativity, outcomes, and impact. John Stott said, "[Jesus'] words and deeds belonged to each other, the words interpreting the deeds and the deeds embodying the words. He did not only announce the good news of the kingdom; he performed visible 'signs of the kingdom.' "[7]

This is why I believe that the mission of the church is community outreach. God came from heaven to earth—God has reached *out*. Therefore, the purpose of the church is to reach *out*—to our family, neighborhoods, and communities for the glory of God, so we can make disciples who will join with us in this missional movement. Perhaps the Holy Spirit convicted Nicholas Wolterstorff to say, "Scripture is the fundamental source for one's speaking with a Christian voice and acting out of Christian conviction."[8]

Let the story of the "four people" be a reminder of our duty and responsibility: "There was an important job to be done, and Everybody was asked to do it. Everybody was sure Somebody would do it. Anybody could have done it, but Nobody did it. Somebody got angry about that, because it was Everybody's job. Everybody thought Anybody could do it, but Nobody realized that Everybody wouldn't do it. It ended up that Everybody blamed Somebody when Nobody did what Anybody could have done."

Again, Why do we exist?

- We are created to serve God and His people.
- We are saved to serve God and His people.
- We are called to serve God and His people.
- We are commissioned to serve God and His people.
- We are commended to serve God and His people.

We are Adventists!

---

1. Quoted in Alan J. Roxburgh and M. Scott Boren, *Introducing the Missional Church: What It Is, Why It Matters, How to Become One* (Grand Rapids, MI: Baker Books, 2009), 20.

2. Darrell L. Guder, *The Continuing Conversion of the Church*, The Gospel and Our Culture Series (Grand Rapids, MI: William B. Eerdmans, 2000), 95, 96.

3. Daniel Joseph and Toby McKeehan, "What If I Stumble?" recorded by DC Talk (Forefront/Virgin Records, 1995).

4. Timothy Keller, *Center Church: Doing Balanced, Gospel-Centered Ministry in Your City* (Grand Rapids, MI: Zondervan, 2012), 284, 285.

5. Alan Kreider, " 'They Alone Know the Right Way to Live': The Early Church and Evangelism," in *Ancient Faith for the Church's Future*, ed. Mark Husbands and Jeffrey P. Greenman (Downers Grove, IL: InterVarsity Press, 2008), 170.

6. Keller, *Center Church*, 285 (italics in the original).

7. John Stott, *Christian Mission in the Modern World* (Downers Grove, IL: InterVarsity Press, 2008), 29.

8. Quoted in Duane Liftin, *Word Versus Deed: Resetting the Scales to a Biblical Balance* (Wheaton, IL: Crossway, 2012), 16.

Acknowledgments

This book is a milestone in my personal life and professional career. I have been fortunate to learn theories and concepts that would have been impossible for me to learn had I not extensively carried out the needed research. I am grateful to a number of people who have guided, supported, and assisted me throughout this process.

I thank my Lord, Jesus Christ, for His mercy and grace over my personal and professional journey. He kept His faithful promise throughout the process and lifted me up every time I failed to continue with passion and commitment.

In addition, a wonderful scholarship from the North American Division administration made it possible for me to pursue a PhD in leadership at Andrews University. They invested in me to enhance my leadership knowledge and skills and to become a more faithful servant of our God.

Yung Mi F. Suh spent countless hours proofreading, editing, and listening to me talk about my research. I can't express enough my sincerest gratitude for her generosity and assistance throughout this great endeavor.

I would like to express my sincere appreciation and grateful heart to my wife, Me Young, who has cheered me on since the beginning of our life together and supported me through the good times and the bad times with unconditional love and grace.

My two children, Teresa and Joshua, helped me along the course of this journey by giving encouragement and providing the moral and emotional support I needed to complete the book.

Finally, thanks goes to my father, who sacrificed so much to immigrate to the United States of America and laid a firm foundation for our family to stand on and grow from. I am eternally grateful for his commitment and love.

Introduction

In my humble opinion, the mission of the church is community outreach. The church exists for this reason. In fact, "mission is not primarily an activity of the church, but an attribute of God. God is a missionary God. . . . Mission is thereby seen as a movement from God to the world; the church is viewed as an instrument for that mission. There is church because there is mission, not vice versa. To participate in mission is to participate in the movement of God's love toward people, since God is a fountain of sending love."[1]

> "Mission is not primarily an activity of the church, but an attribute of God. God is a missionary God."
> —David J. Bosch

God came from heaven to earth; God has reached out. Therefore, we must reach out to our communities if we are to call ourselves Christlike. Ellen White writes, "The church is God's appointed agency for the salvation of men. *It was organized for service, and its mission is to carry the gospel to the world.* From the beginning it has been God's plan that through His church shall be reflected to the world His fullness and His sufficiency. *The members of the church, those whom He has called out of darkness into His marvelous light, are to show forth His glory.*"[2]

So church was organized for service (community outreach); that's why churches are planted. This is why the church cannot be a weekly program, but an expression of how God has reached out to us, first. Thereafter, we cannot come out of the darkness and just stay in His marvelous light; we need to go back into the darkness and be a change agent—a difference-maker. We are chosen by God to be the salt and the light of the world.

As Jesus says in Matthew 20:28, "The Son of Man did not come to be served, but to serve." We are created, saved, called, commissioned, and commanded to serve God and His people. That is our mandate and that is the life that we ought to live, but Anatole France says that "the average man does not know what to do with this life, yet wants another one which will last forever."[3] We don't know what to do with this current life, but we want to go to heaven and live forever.

> "The church is God's appointed agency for the salvation of men. *It was organized for service, and its mission is to carry the gospel to the world."*
> —Ellen G. White

That's why God inspired us with three essential functions of the church to complete its community outreach mission: discipleship, world mission, and community transformation. The church should be equipping, developing, educating, and enlightening disciples (the change agents and difference-makers), and taking the three angels' messages to the ends of the world. And wherever we are in the world, individually or collectively as the Adventist Church body (various congregations, health-care and educational institutions, etc.), the surrounding environs must be different from others, transformed by our faithful presence in the midst of them, as God's servants.

Jesus as our example

We witness the life of Christ at the cross of Calvary—the grand monument of mercy and regeneration, salvation and redemption—when the Son of God was lifted up on the cross.[4] Ellen White says, "The sacrifice of Christ as an atonement for sin is the great truth around which all other truths cluster. In order to be rightly understood and appreciated, every truth in the word of God, from Genesis to Revelation, must be studied in the light that streams from the cross of Calvary."[5] The cross of Calvary is crucial for Christians not only for Christ's death and resurrection, which are the core values of the plan of salvation, but more so for how He lived His life. As His children and His disciples, we must emulate Christ's life.

Jesus lived His life as a humble servant. Therefore, the bottom line of the Christian journey is to be servants of God, by serving His people, not just the "chosen" within the walls of the church building, but by being His disciples outside the walls of the church.

Servanthood is a Christian journey. It is saying, "As true disciples, we are following Jesus all the way," and it is foundational and central to the Christian's life and ministry. Being leading servants is serving *with* Jesus, not just *for* Jesus. Jesus said, "Whoever wants to be my disciple must deny themselves and take up their cross daily and follow me" (Luke 9:23).

Servants *with* Jesus

Servanthood is an essential requirement for a leader. God gave various spiritual gifts to the church (disciples, prophets, teachers, ministers, etc.) regardless of each individual's calling; servanthood is the basis for all gifts that encourages others to serve, to give, to help, to be merciful and hospitable. These traits are even more critical in the church than in the corporate world. As our Lord Jesus Christ served, so ought we to serve one another.[6]

However, we have some challenges. One of them is that we don't want to be servants—we want to be leaders. Rick Warren says, "Thousands of books have been written on leadership, but few on servanthood. Everyone wants to lead; no one wants to be a servant. We would rather be generals than privates. Even Christians want to be *'servant-leaders,'* not just plain servants. But to be like Jesus is to be a servant."[7] Bernice Ledbetter, Robert Banks, and David Greenhalgh discuss the phrase "servant leadership": " 'Leadership' remains the key term and 'servant' the qualifier. What we need today are not, as is so often suggested, more *servant leaders* but, properly understood, more *leading servants*."[8] If we don't have a servant's heart and attitude, we are not qualified to lead.

> "Kneeling in faith at [the foot of] the cross, he [the sinner] has reached the highest place to which man can attain."
> —Ellen G. White

We need more *leading servants* who understand that the gospel must be preached, the lost must be found, the believers must be equipped, the poor must be served, the lonely must be enfolded into community, and God gets the credit for it all.[9] Ellen White writes, "Kneeling in faith at [the foot of] the cross, he [the sinner] has reached the highest place to which man can attain."[10] The highest place is not being a director, president, or CEO; it is at the foot of the cross.

If one does not have a servant's heart and a servant's attitude, it is possible to serve in church for a lifetime without ever being a servant. Leaders who are not real servants first, with a servant's heart, are potentially dangerous. They tend to abuse power and pamper their egos.[11]

They care only about maximizing their pleasure and minimizing their pain and usually end up exercising a leadership style and approach that can be destructive to them and their followers.

The leader must serve the organization and its members. Ask yourself, *Do I think more about others than about myself? Do I base my identity in Christ? Do I think of ministry as an opportunity, not an obligation?* Servanthood is not only serving Jesus but also serving *with* Jesus. It involves not only being servants of Christ, but also being servants *with* Christ. When we serve *for* Christ, we rely on our own knowledge, but when we serve *with* Jesus, we rely on Him and become His instruments.

Demonstrate your love

Throughout Jesus' ministry we witness a genuine servanthood approach toward humanity, especially people who were marginalized, disadvantaged, and disenfranchised from society. They were the poor, the sick, the unclean—all outcasts as sinful people. Jesus expanded the kingdom of God to places, people, and cultures that the Jews had never considered God to be interested in.[12]

Jesus grieved over the multitudes of people who were helpless and brought hope to their lives by ministering to their needs. Through this compassionate service, Jesus was able to build a trust relationship. "Christ's method alone will give true success in reaching the people. The Saviour *mingled* with men as one who *desired* their good. He *showed* His sympathy for them, *ministered* to their needs, and *won* their confidence. Then He bade them, 'Follow Me.' "[13] Jesus mingled with people, identified their needs, met their needs, and through the service relationship, He built a bridge of trust. And then He said to the people, "Follow Me." Christ's method requires a lifetime of commitment to the community, because Christianity is a journey, and it is about establishing a faithful relationship until the second coming of Christ. It is a process—connecting the church with the community. We must earn the right and privilege to share the truth that we have, before we ask them to "follow me."

The purpose of being a disciple is not only to proclaim the good

> "Christ's method alone will give true success in reaching the people. The Saviour *mingled* with men as one who *desired* their good. He *showed* His sympathy for them, *ministered* to their needs, and *won* their confidence. Then He bade them, 'Follow Me.' "
> —Ellen G. White

news, the word of salvation, but also to demonstrate the love of God to people who are in need. "It is God himself who has made us what we are and given us new lives from Christ Jesus; and long ages ago he planned that we should spend these lives in helping others" (Ephesians 2:10, TLB). This is why service is not optional in Christian servanthood. We are called to maintain and improve social conditions of society. We are commanded to create kingdom values in this world. We are commissioned to become change-makers in our communities.

Unfortunately, in their institutional preoccupation, some churches have abandoned their real identity and reason for existence.[14] Like the Sadducees, who were in charge of Jerusalem's temple-based activity, we've sold out to materialism and religious ritual; we've become systematic and mechanical religious practitioners. Like the Pharisees, who held control in the synagogue and dominated the religious agenda, policies, and operational procedures, we've produced a dead religion.

The reality is that in general, people in the community don't care much about organized religious institutions or club memberships. They think that religious people do not see people—they see only causes, behaviors, and stereotypes. And non-Christians think religious people do not react with their hearts, but rather think and act in a calculating way.[15]

In Korea, we say a father's love is logical and a mother's love is emotional. When my son was younger, he would fall and hurt himself often. When this happened, my wife ran after him to see if he was OK and to make sure there were no broken bones. On the other hand, I behaved logically. I watched from a distance, analyzing the circumstances. Then I'd approach him and ask him *why he had fallen*, *how did he fall*, and *what had he learned from the experience*. While my boy was crying out for a hug, I was trying to figure out *why!* Sometimes we do that as a church. People are crying out for the love of God, and the assurance of God's grace, forgiveness, and mercy, but we stand at a distance, trying to figure out why and how they fell.

There are times we Christians are great at speaking the truth without love. We have the truth and know what people desperately need, but the challenge is that people will not receive it from us because we don't *see* people. We see prospects, potential church membership growth opportunities; we approach our communities as fishing pools, and they perceive our (dis)interest, not care.

When was the last time you thought, *How do I turn myself into a missionary? How do I deploy myself as a missionary in a community transformation?* Because we are called into the servanthood of Christianity, we ought to take the gospel to where people are, especially the market-place. Jesus went to the places where the people were. Likewise, we need churches where people are—at the mall, supermarkets, laundromats, schools, places of work, restaurants, coffee shops, and so forth. For the most part, people are not coming to us; we have to go to them. Being a servant requires that we continually adopt new ways of thinking and working. We can't stay inside the walls of the church and shout at the community, "Come and see!" Come and see *what*? We need to take this passive mentality out of the church and be engaged proactively with our communities.

As leading servants, are we making any impact on the communities in which our institutions are located? What about our churches, schools, and hospitals? Are these neighborhoods better places to live because of our existence in these communities? When was the last time that you heard someone from the community say, "I am a better father today because of your church"; "I am a better mother because of your hospital"; or "I am a better person because of your school"? The problem is *not* our inability to do this; it is our *pride* and *our lack of concern for people.* That is a problem God has observed about His people throughout the ages. Because of institu-tionalized, corporate *churchi-anity*, we are often reluctant to be connected with people outside the church. Mother Teresa said, "You can find Calcutta anywhere in the world. You only need two eyes to see. Everywhere in the world there are people that are not loved, people that are not wanted nor desired, people that no one will help, people that are pushed away or forgotten. And this is the greatest poverty."[16] We see people in need everywhere, but the challenge is that we don't see them as God's children; we see ste-reotypes, causes, and external appearances. We need to pray for our eyes to become like God's eyes, to see His children through His loving eyes.

Growing up Christian, we have been taught and trained to sell our brand of religion. We are so intent on convincing people that their lives are messed up, their faith is wrong, and their beliefs are incorrect that we overlook the fact that we are unskilled at listening to and engaging

> "You can find Calcutta anywhere in the world. You only need two eyes to see. Everywhere in the world there are people that are not loved, people that are not wanted nor desired, people that no one will help, people that are pushed away or forgotten. And this is the greatest poverty."
> —Mother Teresa

people.[17] We often look at them as *prospects* for membership, rather than as spiritual beings with the same need for God that we have. We need to stop training people as mechanics to work within the church industry and instead equip and develop them to become disciples for the kingdom of God, as leading servants to turn "the world upside down" (Acts 17:6, NKJV). We need to shift from *going to* church at a clubhouse to *being* a church in the world. We are human *beings*; therefore, the church must become a *being*, instead of just a place to go.

We must pray for God's intervention in our lives and listen to people's struggles and challenges, looking for an opportunity to serve and demonstrate the love of God. When we intentionally and sincerely approach people who are disenfranchised, disassociated, and marginalized in our communities, we will witness changes in their lives—and changes in our communities. The problem isn't an individual *ability*, but *availability*.

Leading servants are Christian disciples who order their lives around missionary purpose and who believe they are responsible for fulfilling the Great Commission.[18] Their organization is not hierarchical, but rather a flat circle. They measure their effectiveness and impact of ministry beyond the walls of the church by asking:

How is our dependability—are we doing what we say we will do?

How is our timeliness—are we doing it when we say we will do it?

How is our empathy—are we helping, with an eye to the needs of community?

What is our tangible evidence—are we doing our service in ways that let communities know their needs have been met?

As we serve the community through Christ's love and faith in action, Christians will demonstrate what it means to be a leading servant, and we will begin to knock down the barriers between churches and communities. This is why community outreach is both proclaiming the good news and demonstrating God's love and concern for every soul. The bottom line is that we are called to servanthood in discipleship. When we say we are Christians, we are not talking about *self-serving* Christianity, but *other-serving* Christianity—Jesus' serving disciples.[19] When we place others before us and above us, we will begin to practice the values and principles of Christianity.

Bill Hybels says that Christ through the church is "the hope of the world," and I believe that servants are the hope of the kingdom of God.[20] God has called us to servanthood; this is nonnegotiable. We follow Jesus in humble and loving service, as He Himself was the humble

Servant. By Christ's model of compassionate service and love, we can lead people to spiritual transformation, and then transform the world for the kingdom of God on earth, as it is in heaven.

---

1. David J. Bosch, *Transforming Mission: Paradigm Shifts in Theology of Mission*, 20th anniversary edition, American Society of Missiology Series, no. 16 (1991; repr., Maryknoll, NY: Orbis Books, 2011), 400.

2. Ellen G. White, *The Acts of the Apostles* (Mountain View, CA: Pacific Press®, 1911), 9 (emphasis added).

3. Anatole France, https://www.great-quotes.com/quote/122613.

4. Michael Horton, *The Gospel Commission: Recovering God's Strategy for Making Disciples* (Grand Rapids, MI: Baker Books, 2011).

5. Ellen G. White, *Gospel Workers* (Washington, DC: Review and Herald®, 1915), 315.

6. Siang-Yang Tan, *Full Service: Moving From Self-Serve Christianity to Total Servanthood* (Grand Rapids, MI: Baker Books, 2006).

7. Rick Warren, *The Purpose Driven Life: What on Earth Am I Here For?* (Grand Rapids, MI: Zondervan, 2002), 257, 258 (italics in the original).

8. Bernice M. Ledbetter, Robert J. Banks, and David C. Greenhalgh, *Reviewing Leadership: A Christian Evaluation of Current Approaches*, 2nd ed., Engaging Culture (Grand Rapids, MI: Baker Academic, 2016), 109 (italics in the original).

9. Richard Stearns, *The Hole in Our Gospel: The Answer That Changed My Life and Might Just Change the World* (Nashville, TN: Thomas Nelson, 2009).

10. White, *Acts of the Apostles*, 210.

11. Tan, *Full Service*.

12. Harvie M. Conn and Manuel Ortiz, *Urban Ministry: The Kingdom, the City, and the People of God* (Downers Grove, IL: InterVarsity Press, 2001).

13. Ellen G. White, *The Ministry of Healing* (Mountain View, CA: Pacific Press®, 1942), 143 (emphasis added).

14. Brenda Salter McNeil and Rick Richardson, *The Heart of Racial Justice: How Soul Change Leads to Social Change*, expanded ed. (Downers Grove, IL: IVP Books, 2009).

15. Ronald J. Sider, Philip N. Olson, and Heidi Rolland Unruh, *Churches That Make a Difference: Reaching Your Community With Good News and Good Works* (Grand Rapids, MI: Baker Books, 2002).

16. Mother Teresa, https://www.goodreads.com/quotes/658204-you-can-find-calcutta -anywhere-in-the-world-you-only.

17. Kevin DeYoung and Ted Kluck, *Why We Love the Church: In Praise of Institutions and Organized Religion* (Chicago: Moody Publishers, 2009).

18. Kevin DeYoung and Greg Gilbert, *What Is the Mission of the Church? Making Sense of Social Justice, Shalom, and the Great Commission* (Wheaton, IL: Crossway, 2011).

19. Philip Jenkins, *The Next Christendom: The Coming of Global Christianity*, 3rd ed. (New York: Oxford University Press, 2011).

20. Bill Hybels, *The Volunteer Revolution: Unleashing the Power of Everybody* (Grand Rapids, MI: Zondervan, 2004), 32.

PART I:

WHY—Why Do We Do What We Do?

CHAPTER 1

Why Do We Exist?

The great calling: God is Creator, Redeemer, and Judge

We sometimes ponder the three most fundamental questions of life:

1. Who am I?
2. Where did I come from?
3. What is my destiny?

Which question is most important? In my humble opinion, the key question is the second one: *Where did I come from?* Based on that answer, you will know who you are and what your destiny is all about.

God has chosen us to be a royal priesthood—that is our mandate. "You are a chosen people, a royal priesthood, a holy nation, God's special possession, that you may declare the praises of him who called you out of darkness into his wonderful light" (1 Peter 2:9). God has not chosen us to become kings nor prophets. I know some of us would like to be a king or a prophet, but God has chosen us as a priesthood/ servants. By definition, a priest does two things: *serves God* and *serves God's people.*

Therefore, I personally feel the fundamental question is not *Who am I?* but *To* whom *do I belong?*—because that defines *who we are* in this world. We belong to God, and we were created, saved, called, commissioned, and commanded to serve—serve God, and serve His people.

Sometimes as Christians, we have a great understanding of the Word of God; we have lots of theology—head knowledge and head faith. But the head is not connected to the heart, which should have a passion for God's mission and a passion to serve, and our hearts are not connected to our hands—to demonstrate our commitment and love for God and His people. This is why non-Christians say to Christians, "Christians don't live in reality." We just blow hot air; we talk about the love of God, but in reality, that love doesn't exist. And that's why we need to ponder our values and principles. Jesus says that "as the Father has sent me, so I send you" (John 20:21, NRSV). That's why our mandate is to go where people are and make a difference.

In fact, during the first century in the book of Acts, you see this great movement begin and evolve. People from Hellenistic backgrounds, Samaritans, Romans, and Gentiles come together and start a revenant movement: Christendom.

The Pharisees and Sadducees begin to ridicule them by saying they are dangerous people, that they are a contagious disease. Christians are about to turn the world upside down. "These who have turned the world upside down have come here too" (Acts 17:6, NKJV). The Pharisees misinterpreted God's mission, but they called this movement perfectly: Christians are contagious and we turn the world upside down for the kingdom of God, on this earth, as it is in heaven. That's why we exist.

But sometimes we come to church week after week and systematically and mechanically participate in a religious ritual. We become religious practitioners instead of living our lives as disciples. We pray every day for the kingdom of God to be a reality on earth, as it is in heaven (Matthew 6:10). But is that true?

That's why I believe God has called us to carry out the mission of turning the world upside down. God has called us to proclaim the three angels' messages, that beautiful everlasting good news: God is the Creator, the Redeemer, and the Judge. Ellen White writes, "The sacrifice of Christ as an atonement for sin is the great truth around which all other truths cluster. In order to be rightly understood and appreciated, every truth in the word of God, from Genesis to Revelation, must be studied in the light that streams from the cross of Calvary."[1]

The cross of Calvary is our focus; it's where we see not only the death and resurrection of Jesus Christ, but how He lived His life. Yes, the death and resurrection of Jesus is one of the core values of our belief, but we must see how He lived on *from* the cross of Calvary. Instead, we have developed a displacement culture and understanding between the kingdom of God (kingdom of grace) and the kingdom of heaven (kingdom of glory). We say, "This is not my world; we are going home (heaven)," but while we sing and talk about it on earth, we only care for two things: maximizing our pleasure and minimizing our pain. "Who cares about people dying from hunger, the sick, and the imprisoned, as long as my life is satisfying and I'm content? That's all I care about." And so we say, "This is not my world; we are just passing through." Perhaps this is why non-Christians say Christians are hypocrites. Because we are not being real.

We will be in the kingdom of heaven through the sacrifice of Christ, but we have a responsibility and duty in this kingdom of God *today*. We are living in the kingdom of grace on earth *today*, and we must be faithful to our duty and responsibility in this world *today*, as we practice for living in the kingdom of heaven tomorrow. Our focus should not be the kingdom of heaven alone, or the kingdom of glory, but being faithful in the kingdom of God by fulfilling our duty and responsibilities.

Christianity is a journey with God. Unfortunately, God's people don't always understand the journey, and that's what was happening in Luke 17:20, 21. The Pharisees came to Jesus and asked *when* the kingdom of God was coming. But Jesus implies that the focus is not when, but *where* the kingdom is . . . today: "Now having been questioned by the Pharisees as to when the kingdom of God was coming, He answered them and said, 'The kingdom of God is not coming with signs to be observed; nor will they say, "Look, here it is!" or, "There it is!" For behold, the kingdom of God is in your midst' " (Luke 17:20, 21, NASB). The New Century Version of the Bible says, "God's kingdom is within you" (v. 21, NCV). Jesus was talking about Himself and also us, the disciples of God. Jesus is the kingdom of God, and the kingdom is not here or there; it's within us. The focus is not *when* the kingdom of God will occur, but *where* the kingdom of God is today. As a result of our faithful presence individually and collectively as a church, have we made a difference in our community as a part of the kingdom of God on earth?

After forty days in the wilderness, Jesus went into the synagogue and read:

> "The Spirit of the Lord is on me,
>   because he has anointed me
>   to proclaim good news to the poor.
> He has sent me to proclaim freedom for the prisoners
>   and recovery of sight for the blind,
> to set the oppressed free,
>   to proclaim the year of the Lord's favor."

Then he rolled up the scroll, gave it back to the attendant and sat down. The eyes of everyone in the synagogue were fastened on him. He began by saying to them, "Today this scripture is fulfilled in your hearing." (Luke 4:18–21)

Basically, He said all the things you have heard right now are done—finished.

And what was the result of hearing what Jesus said? "All the people in the synagogue were furious when they heard this. They got up, drove him out of the town, and took him to the brow of the hill on which the town was built, in order to throw him off the cliff" (vv. 28, 29). The Greek for *furious* implies mad enough to kill. After He read the scripture and said it "is fulfilled," people got upset. They took Him and intended to throw Him off a cliff. They decided to kill the Messiah.

What went wrong on this Sabbath? He was in church reading the Bible. Why would they kill Jesus? They had developed their own theology of hope. It was their own eschatology that made them decide to kill the Messiah.

Isaiah 61 is a Messianic mission statement and a sacred scripture. Traditionally, those with prestige, status, and high standing would read chapter 61. Jesus was a son of a carpenter, He wasn't even educated in a seminary and had not obtained any credentials behind His name, and He was reading this sacred scripture. Then, while reading Isaiah 61, He said "recovery of sight for the blind," which is not in Isaiah 61. He was adding to the scripture—this was blasphemous. He was a nobody, had no authority, dared to read Isaiah 61, and He was adding to the scripture. We know Jesus is the author of the entire Bible and He has the right to do it, but to that audience, He had no right.

Then He did the unthinkable once again; He didn't even bother reading what they considered the most important part of Isaiah: "and the day of vengeance of our God" (Isaiah 61:2). He ended it at "to proclaim the year of the Lord's favor." Most Jews, especially the Pharisees, didn't care about preaching the good news to the poor, binding up the brokenhearted, freedom for the captives, or providing release for people from darkness—no, they only focused on the day of God's vengeance.

They thought, *When the Messiah comes, the Romans will be out, the Gentiles will be out, and the Samaritans will be out. We will restore the nation of Israel once again.* But Jesus didn't even bother to read that. He read "proclaim the year of the Lord's favor." This is known as the year of jubilee. "Consecrate the fiftieth year and proclaim liberty throughout the land to all its inhabitants. It shall be a jubilee for you; each of you is to return to your family property and to your own clan" (Leviticus 25:10). Every fifty years the land was to be returned to the rightful owner. All debt was to be cleared. If you were a slave, you were freed from your slavery. This was a social justice system, a personal justice system, a reset button that God had installed every fifty years for humanity's benefit. But during the time between Malachi and John the Baptist—four hundred years—they did not practice the year of jubilee. They replaced God's law with their own inclinations; instead of observing God's will, they developed their own ways of keeping the Sabbath holy.

So during the four hundred years, they developed their own theology of hope, if I might say eschatology, by saying that when the Messiah came, the year of jubilee would be "the sign" of the time. So when Jesus said, "Today this scripture is fulfilled," they looked around at one another and said, "I'm still a slave." "I'm still in debt; I still owe a lot of money." "What do you mean give my land back to the rightful landowner? I worked hard for this land. I'm not going to give it up."

They labeled Him a false prophet, not the real Messiah. They decided to kill Jesus right there. Because of their own theology of hope, their own end-time understanding, they missed the whole point of the Messianic missional statement, which was *The proclamation of the good news of salvation, compassion for the sick and the sorrowful, and a majestic commitment to justice.*

Today we have the same tendency. We focus on *when* and we miss *where* the kingdom of God is today. We spend more time trying to figure out how close we are to the second coming of Christ than focusing on experiencing the kingdom of God in our lives *right now!* Because of that focus, we are not teaching and practicing the kingdom values and principles; instead we focus on rules and regulations.

For instance, we do not spend money on the Sabbath. Why? Is it because we have spent on the last six days? If that is your rationale, then why drive on the Sabbath? You should walk instead of driving. Instead of eating on the Sabbath, we should be fasting and praying. Perhaps we should stay home and play dead or have meditation with "Saint Mattress." Here is my understanding: we do not spend money on the Sabbath because of jubilee—kingdom values and principles, the social justice system, which God installed in humanity. When rich and poor do not spend money on the Sabbath, it shows that we are all equal— created equal by God, equal in the eyes of our God and in the eyes of our society. It demonstrates social equality, personal equity, and liberation, a weekly reminder of the kingdom values and principles that we must teach and practice. Through Christian social and personal justice, we must be engaged and involved in transformative social action, civic engagement for equality, equity, liberation, and civic responsibility.

Based on that understanding, we must seek the second coming of Christ *from* the cross of Calvary. It will change our perspectives regarding the second coming of Christ. We're not working toward victory, but working *from* the victory. We're not working toward salvation, but working *from* salvation. That's why salvation is not something to obtain, but to retain. This is why it has been said, "Salvation is Jesus Christ—period, and plus nothing!"

M. Craig Barnes says, "We killed Jesus, not because he claimed to be the Messiah but because he became like us. That is a blasphemy against our greatest hopes for what a messiah will do. We don't want a savior who descends into our humanity. We want a savior who will rescue us from all the judgments we have faced."[2]

> "*Discover Grace.* Our hope is that when people discover grace—Christ and God's gift of grace through the cross—that they will have an eternity change. *Grow in Grace.* We also hope that we can help them grow in understanding that grace. As a result of knowing Christ, we want them to have a life change. *Live Gracefully.* We also want them to get engaged in living out grace—to find ways to serve and allow grace to show up in how they live. We want to help them change their part of the world."
>
> —Rick Rusaw

Perhaps we have similar challenges understanding the Messiah's missional heart. We keep forgetting the cross of Calvary is the first and foremost reason for our existence, and therefore we're not fulfilling our responsibility in this world. Through the cross of Calvary we see and hear the good news—the three angels' messages, which talk about God who is the Creator of the entire universe and mankind, including the Sabbath day; the God who delivered us from our bondage as the Redeemer; the God who delivered us from the darkness of Babylon into His marvelous light; the God who is the Judge full of amazing grace and mercy. In fact, our focus should not be limited to "How will I be judged?" but "*Who* is the judge and *what is my relationship* with the judge?" We belong to God, who is the Creator, Redeemer, and Judge.

We are His. That is why the three angels' messages are good news, the everlasting gospel. We must be liberated from the fear of judgment and discover the graceful and merciful Judge, and live accordingly.

Pastor Rick Rusaw from the LifeBridge Christian Church explains the importance of grace in a meaningful and relevant way:

> *Discover Grace.* Our hope is that when people discover grace—Christ and God's gift of grace through the cross—that they will have an eternity change. *Grow in Grace.* We also hope that we can help them grow in understanding that grace. As a result of knowing Christ, we want them to have a life change. *Live Gracefully.* We also want them to get engaged in living out grace—to find ways to serve and allow grace to show up in how they live. We want to help them change their part of the world.[3]

The Great Commission: evangelist and disciple

Isaiah 61 is the Messianic job description, and Isaiah 58 is *our* job description as Christians. But we often focus on verses 13 and 14 in chapter 58 and ignore the rest of our job description. When you have a job, you are obligated to fulfill your entire job description—it's mandatory that you fulfill all aspects of your job, not just the parts that you like, or you get fired. And the entire chapter of Isaiah 58 is our job description.

In verses 1–5, God's people are criticized for making God's work about themselves. In verses 6–11, God defines true fasting, which was misunderstood. Perhaps we are supposedly fasting in remembrance of people who do not have food to eat. For now, let's focus on Isaiah 58:12:

> Your people will rebuild the ancient ruins
> and will raise up the age-old foundations;
> you will be called *Repairer* of Broken Walls,
> *Restorer* of Streets with Dwellings (emphasis added).

God has chosen us to become repairers and restorers. When you look at the Hebrew word for repair (*gadar*), it implies we are here to reconnect the broken relationship between God and His people. And God has said we are restorers (*schuwb*), which implies to turn back, to change societal values with His kingdom values. We are change agents—difference-makers.

"Therefore go and make disciples of all nations, baptizing them in the name of the Father and of the Son and of the Holy Spirit, and teaching them to obey everything I have commanded you. And surely I am with you always, to the very end of the age" (Matthew 28:19, 20)—this is called the Great Commission. When we baptize people in the name of the Father, the Son, and the Holy Spirit, are we being restorers or repairers? We are being repairers. We are reconnecting people to God, reconciling their broken relationship. We are not just getting people wet in the institutional initiation; we are baptizing them into this beautiful relationship with God. That's why we proclaim the three angels' messages.

Then when we "go and make disciples of all nations, . . . teaching them," we are being restorers. We are enlightening, educating, developing, and equipping change agents—difference-makers. We are connecting people with God and His people.

As repairers and restorers, we have challenges. The first challenge is to *go*—go where God's people are. But we often hide inside the walls of the church, and we say to the rest of the world, "Come and see." Come and see *what*? God says, "Go to where My people are." We have developed a passive attitude regarding community outreach, and we do not proactively engage with the community, which exists outside the walls of the church.

The second challenge is to "make disciples"—enlighten, educate, develop, and equip. But we love to train people to become robotic, to work within the church industry. We operate our church as a Henry Ford automobile assembly line. Because we have adopted an industrial model of organizational behavior, we become religiously institutionalized, a corporate churchianity. For example, we love to use such words as *training*. But we shouldn't train people in the church—we should *enlighten people. We should develop and educate people in the church for discipleship.* My opposition is not so much with the word *training*, but with the attitude behind the word. Church is not an institution, which requires people to be trained to learn a specific skill, such as the military or the medical field or assembly industries. Church is about having a journey with Christ and His followers, through the lifelong process of mentoring and coaching individuals to become more mature followers of Christ, and becoming disciples who follow His instructions with greater conceptual and analytical skills. That's why the early Jewish society expected Jesus to invest at least three years with His disciples. If you spent any less time with your rabbi, then society didn't recognize you as his disciple. How can we develop disciples, these change agents, by electing new local church officials every year or two? This is not effective.

Through the transitional leadership change, we tend to focus on developing technical skills to do the job. However, discipleship requires transformational leadership development, focusing not only on technical skills, but also on human relationship and analytical skills to lead the church and be a difference-maker in our communities. We must stop training people to practice only technical aspects of ministry and begin to engage in developing disciples to learn conceptual and analytical skills, and competencies. (I will discuss this topic in more detail in chapter 6.)

The third challenge is "all nations." When Jesus cleansed the temple and cast out the merchants, He reclaimed the temple as "a house of prayer for all nations" (Mark 11:17). The Sadducees decided to kill Jesus right then and there for two reasons: finances and theology. When Jesus cast out the merchants, the Sadducees lost their financial endowment. And they didn't like Jesus calling the temple a house of prayer for all nations. To the Sadducees, the temple was only for the Jews, the Israelites, or Sabbatarians. In their minds, there was no room for Samaritans, Romans, or foreigners in the kingdom of God. That's why they decided to kill Jesus. But Jesus said the kingdom of God is for all nations.

You probably assume I go to a Korean church. We all look alike (to some people). We all talk alike, behave alike, and eat alike—it could be a really boring church (to some people). Nevertheless, the kingdom of God is for all nations. Wherever your church is located, your church membership needs to reflect your immediate community. If your church membership does not reflect your own community, there is something wrong with your church. If people in your community are not attending your church, in my humble opinion, your church is not "being a church."

African American, Asian, Hispanic, or Caucasian—your church membership must reflect your immediate communities. It can't be just a place you go once a week for your cliquish social gathering. This is why the Great Commission is given to us. To proclaim the gospel to *everyone*, not just to the ones who look like us. And to baptize people in the name of the Father, the Son, and the Holy Spirit. We must serve in harmony; teach and obey everything Jesus has taught us; care for the physical, mental, social, and spiritual needs—the whole person—and witness to our neighbors.

Repairer	Restorer
Evangelist	Disciple
To proclaim the good news	To demonstrate the love of God

If I reframe the aforementioned, we are repairers, restoring the broken people with God, reconnecting their relationship with God and their family, neighborhood, community, and so forth; therefore, we are *evangelists*, and our duty and responsibility is to proclaim the good news. As restorers, we are difference-makers, servants of our God; therefore, we are *disciples*, and our mandate is to demonstrate the love of God. It's not either/or; we don't have a choice. Every single one of us is an evangelist and a disciple.

Every time I travel, I do three things religiously at the airport. I pray for the pilot, to make sure he or she will take us from point A to point B without crashing us to the ground. I pray for the mechanics, to make sure they do their job flawlessly so we don't have any mechanical failures. And third, I check to make sure the plane has two wings, because that plane will not fly with only one wing.

And as a Christian, every single one of us must have two wings. We must be repairers and restorers. We must be evangelists and disciples. We must proclaim the good news and demonstrate the love of God. Regardless of whether you are young or old, male or female—it doesn't make a difference. Every single one of us is commissioned by God to be an evangelist *and* a disciple. Wherever we are, whomever we are—individually and collectively.

We shouldn't say, "I'm not a pastor or elder; preaching the good news or conducting an evangelistic meeting is a job for the evangelist." Everyone is commissioned to proclaim the good news; there is no excuse. Some of us practice a dichotomous model of two separate gospels—the evangelical gospel versus the social gospel. "I can do community service, but I can't do the job of the evangelist." There is no compartmentalization or sectioning of the gospel. We have to proclaim the good news *and* demonstrate the love of God. But sometimes we act like the Israelites, who forgot why they were chosen and their chosen status. We are chosen by God to be a part of His great plan of salvation, and it is our greatest honor and privilege to be His instruments. We are chosen and we are commissioned to proclaim the good news and demonstrate the love of God. This is nonnegotiable. It is an obligatory requirement as a child of God. This is what we signed up for when we chose to follow Christ.

The great commandment: Love God, and love your neighbor

Jesus said, " 'Love the Lord your God with all your heart and with all your soul and with all your mind.' This is the first and greatest commandment. And the second is like it: 'Love your neighbor as yourself' " (Matthew 22:37–39). Because God first loved us, we can love—love Him and love His creation (see 1 John 4:19). Out of our love for God, we are to love our neighbors. We are called to live justly and show mercy, to defend righteousness, to live wisely and compassionately, to serve our neighbors. "If anyone has material possessions and sees a brother or sister in need but has no pity on them, how can the love of God be in that person?" (1 John 3:17).

A friend of mine went to Africa to conduct evangelistic meetings. During the weeks, he got to know the chief of the village, and at the end of the third week, with a degree of supercilious pride and ego, he asked, "What did you think of my sermon?" The chief replied, "Well, I hear a lot of thunder . . . but no rain."

Sometimes, that's exactly how our Christian life looks to outsiders— we blow hot air. We *say* we are a loving church, we are about forgiveness, assurances, and hope in His mercy and grace, but look at our behavior. I have visited churches that are so cold I can ice-skate down the aisle.

We act like the priests and Levites when passing by a dying man, and we say, "If I stop to help this man, what will happen to me?" It's all about me! But the Samaritan passes by and asks, "If I don't stop and help this man, what will happen to him?" That's Christianity. When we begin to put others before and above us, we will begin to live like Christ and exude our belief and God's principles.

Christianity is not about *What do I get?* We need to put others above us. Jesus came and died for us, not because we deserved Him, but because we needed Him. There are so many people dying every day not knowing who God is, not experiencing His love and mercy. They may seem to not want Him, but they need Him. This is why we proclaim the good news and demonstrate the love of God.

So the question is not *Who is my neighbor?* The fundamental question is *Am I being a neighbor? Am I being a neighbor to all people, all the time—not just on Sabbath morning?*

Honestly, we're not the real us on Sabbath morning. We go to church once a week; we dress up and behave gently. We will know who we are after the Sabbath. Are we still committed servants of God the rest of the week, every moment of our lives? Or are we rehearsing religion like the Pharisees and Sadducees, as religious practitioners?

"Jesus went through all the towns and villages, teaching in their synagogues, proclaiming the good news of the kingdom and healing every
disease and sickness" (Matthew 9:35). This is who we are. We don't just
look for events, but we live out His example daily. Someone said, "The
church begins when the worship ends."

My friend once said, "Christianity is a great lifestyle," but I took is-
sue with that. Christianity is *not* a great lifestyle—Christianity is life! If
Christianity is simply a lifestyle, then we would be Christians without
Christ.

"For I was hungry, while you had all you needed. I was thirsty, but you drank bottled water. I was a stranger, and you wanted me deported. I needed clothes, but you needed *more* clothes. I was sick, and you pointed out the behaviors that led to my sickness. I was in prison, and you said I was getting what I deserved."

—Richard Stearns

We are change agents.
We are evangelists and disciples at any given moment
of our lives. "Therefore, as
we have opportunity, let us
do good to all people, especially to those who belong
to the family of believers"
(Galatians 6:10).

To promote social justice,
Jesus speaks in the Psalms,

Defend the weak and the fatherless;
    uphold the cause of the poor and the oppressed.
Rescue the weak and the needy;
    deliver them from the hand of the wicked (Psalm 82:3, 4).

This is the reason why we ought to be the voice of the voiceless, the
defender of those who can't defend themselves. But we often hide inside
the walls of the church and say, "We are a loving church. Come and see."

Perhaps this is why Richard Stearns wrote this passage, based on
Matthew 24 and 25: "For I was hungry, while you had all you needed.
I was thirsty, but you drank bottled water. I was a stranger, and you
wanted me deported. I needed clothes, but you needed *more* clothes. I
was sick, and you pointed out the behaviors that led to my sickness. I
was in prison, and you said I was getting what I deserved."[4]

Michael Horton indicates that the ministry of the church is an institution or embassy instituted by Christ; it should be identified by
preaching, baptizing, communing, and teaching everything Christ
taught us. Church is where disciples are made. Worldly vocations are
where disciples are sent.[5]

The most important identity is not being a teacher, lawyer, doctor, farmer, or plumber—those are secondary identities. The foremost identity is that you are Christ's disciple. You are His faithful servant. That's why you are obligated to proclaim the good news and demonstrate the love of God. But most of us still don't get it.

When you have a passive message such as "Come and see," all you care about is having a weekly worship service, the highest goal being an attractive church. And then, we go to church mechanically and systematically. We see the community as a fishing pool. We don't see people; we only see the prospects of possible church membership. We don't see the precious souls that belong to God, because we only care about growing the congregation.

While I was living in Dayton, Ohio, I was privileged to plant a new Korean congregation there and serve as an interim pastor. There were a few interracial married couples within a small Korean population of about two hundred. There weren't a lot of professionals at that time— no lawyers, but a few doctors. Our members went to the hospital or the courts and translated for people who were in need of that service.

One day I got a call from county court about a man who had been arrested while driving under the influence. It was his third time, so he was going to prison for six months and had to pay a fine of five thousand dollars. Our appointment was for one o'clock, so I got there at twelve thirty. But the defendant showed up at one thirty. And when he showed up, he was clearly intoxicated. I couldn't believe it! He was about to go to prison for being drunk and had to pay a fine. Yet he showed up late and drunk again.

This is the point: Every time I went to an appointment like this, I would carry cards with my contact information and directions to the church. Usually after such an appointment, I encouraged the person to contact me and visit our church. And while I was translating for this defendant, I felt the card in my pocket. So while my left brain was translating for him, my right brain was contemplating whether to share my contact information with him or not. In the end, I chose not to share my contact information with him.

I was more concerned about *my* church, *my* new congregation, and *my* children. I didn't want this drunkard coming to contaminate our newly planted congregation. Because I was not looking at him as a precious soul belonging to God, I was looking at his qualification and my standards. And too often we do that because we don't see people as God's children. Sometimes we see them only as a project or prospects for church membership growth because we don't focus on *saving people*—but only on *winning souls for baptism.*

That's why we have to change our perspective from "Come and see" to "Come and be with Christ." Become a disciple and be equipped to be change agents; create a church where difference-makers are educated. Our immediate community wherever we are must be different from the world. It must be the kingdom of God on earth, as it is in heaven. And taking the three angels' messages to the ends of the earth—that is a church.

There is a Seventh-day Adventist church in Paradise Valley, California, that, because of the complexity of environments and people moving away, was declining. Meanwhile, people from all over the world come to Paradise Valley as refugees, and the community has greatly changed. When the church members began to reach out to the community holistically, the church benefited, and it continues to grow in numbers.

By providing simple health screenings, clothing distributions, community gardens, English as a Second Language (ESL) classes, a food pantry, a thrift ministry, transportation, and interacting with the community, the church provided services that were needed by the community. Within five years, they baptized more than 350 souls, and they continue to make a huge difference. When we focus on how to save people, we will win souls as a by-product. And our church will benefit and grow. Church is about *saving people*, not just *winning souls.* God wins souls as we help people through their physical, mental, social, and spiritual challenges.

This is why I believe God has called us, commissioned us, and commanded us to change the world—to turn the world upside down. "These that have turned the world upside down are come hither also" (Acts 17:6, KJV).

John MacArthur said, "The Christian life is not adding Jesus to one's own way of life but renouncing that personal way of life for His and being willing to pay whatever cost that may require."[6] We need to remember, "I have been crucified with Christ and I no longer live, but Christ lives in me. The life I now live in the body, I live by faith in the Son of God, who loved me and gave himself for me" (Galatians 2:20).

> "The Christian life is not adding Jesus to one's own way of life but renouncing that personal way of life for His and being willing to pay whatever cost that may require."
>
> —John MacArthur

Pray that God helps you to be a missionary. Pray God helps you to be a faithful servant. Pray God helps you to be a difference-maker. Stearns interprets what Jesus commanded us to do in Matthew 28:19, 20: "Go, do what I've told you to do, teach what I've taught you to teach, act as I've taught you to act, and love as I've shown you to love. Build my kingdom in all the nations. This is what you were made to do."[7]

Let's be evangelists and disciples!

1. White, *Gospel Workers*, 315.

2. M. Craig Barnes, *When God Interrupts: Finding New Life Through Unwanted Change* (Downers Grove, IL: IVP Books, 2009), Kindle edition, chap. 4.

3. Eric Swanson and Rick Rusaw, *The Externally Focused Quest: Becoming the Best Church for the Community* (San Francisco: Jossey-Bass, 2010), 68.

4. Stearns, *Hole in Our Gospel*, 59 (italics in the original).

5. Michael Horton, *The Gospel Commision: Recovering God's Strategy for Making Disciples* (Grand Rapids, MI: Baker Books, 2011), 231, 232.

6. John MacArthur, *Matthew 8-15*, The MacArthur New Testament Commentary (Chicago: Moody Press, 1987), 24.

7. Richard E. Stearns, *Unfinished: Believing Is Only the Beginning* (Nashville, TN: Thomas Nelson, 2013), 52.

CHAPTER 2

Inevitable Holistic Ministry Engagement

As you understand the missional concept of engaging with the community, I hope you begin to contemplate God's greatest calling, commission, and commandment as the purpose of our existence. This chapter will cover the biblical methodology—the way we reach out to the community, using the biblical framework.

We are chosen by God to be servants—to serve God and His people. And that's why we are chosen as priests. "Just as the Son of Man did not come to be served, but to serve, and to give his life as a ransom for many" (Matthew 20:28). This is our mandate. This is our responsibility. The church was organized for this service—to serve God and to serve His people. This is why community outreach is not just an activity of the church, but also an attribute of our God. Our God is a missionary God; therefore, we must be the expression of God's missional heart on the earth, by proclaiming the good news and demonstrating the love of God.

What is our mission? Why do we exist?
What is the purpose of our existence?
Whenever I visit a church, I look for a few things: their core values, vision, and mission statements, and of course, the bathroom (when you've got to go, you've got to go). The reality is that most churches don't have a clearly defined mission/vision statement based on their core values. Sometimes (at most churches), they just list the Ten Commandments, the fourth commandment, or a list of the 28 fundamental beliefs.

At a church that I once visited, I asked an elder, "What is the mission statement of your church?"

He said, "We believe what the General Conference believes."

So I asked him, "Well then, please tell me, what does the General Conference believe?"

He said, "They believe what we believe." We laugh about it, but it was an unfortunate conversation regarding the mission of the local church.

At other churches I've visited, their mission statement says, "XYZ church, proclaiming the three angels' messages in Revelation 14." And that's it—that is their mission statement. If I wasn't a Christian and I've never read the Bible, I wouldn't understand what I just read. I get the "XYZ church" part. But, what are the three angels' messages? What is Revelation 14?

Oftentimes we talk among ourselves inside the walls of the church, and we don't have a clearly defined mission that we can reveal to the people outside the walls. And if we don't communicate that purpose clearly, outside the walls of the church, how do we exist and become an influence in our communities?

In addition to searching for their core values, vision, and mission statements, I also like to study their church bulletins to estimate the percentage of activities and financial resources allocated for inner-focused church programs versus community outreach programs. In my observation of the churches I have visited, it appears 90 percent of our church activities are inward focused, compared to 10 percent or less, if any, for community outreach ministries. I am not saying that inward-focused ministries are not important. In fact, we must strategically engage in discipleship development ministries. We must mentor and coach people to grow in Christlikeness. We must equip, educate, and develop disciples who will make disciples. But if we solely focus on having busy programs or church activities without a disciple-making focus, I think these inward-focused church activities are a problem.

We should not simply be an educational church, where we invest most of our time and resources into developing head faith, "a pastoral-educational focus with a classroom methodology"; or an attractional church, which focuses on events to entertain people; or even an organic/home church where all we care about is the current members of the group just having "fellowship."[1]

Most community outreach ministries are engaged in sporadic activities, based on eventful projects. We are Adventist, but sometimes we behave as *Event*ists. We love to focus on and do events; except, one event is not connected to the next event. We do isolated events without developing a long-term sustainable community engagement. Please don't misunderstand my argument about events. I am not criticizing the importance of having events and group activities. My concern is that we should not be having events for the sake of an activity, but that each event should be a part of the long-term commitment of community outreach ministries. Each event should be connected to the next event to enhance the quality of the ministry and to fulfill the mission and vision of the church, at all aspects of the Seventh-day Adventist Church, including the ecclesiastical components, health care, and educational institutions intentionally.

How do we create a faithful presence of the Adventist Church in our immediate communities? How do we create a lasting impact through sustainable community development and outreach ministries? How could we demonstrate our dependability and trustworthiness as an integral part of the community? How could we earn the right and privilege to share our beliefs? The solution is Christ's method: personal engagement and building relationships with people in our communities—evangelistic, incarnational, contextual, communal, and reciprocal holistic ministry.

"Relationships are the method. Jesus invited people into relationships with himself; he loved them and in the process showed them how to follow God. His primary method was life-on-life."

—Jim Putnam

Christ's method of community outreach

Jesus Christ grieved over the multitudes of people who were helpless, and He brought hope to their lives by ministering to their needs. Through His compassionate service, Jesus was able to build a trust relationship. Ellen White summarized the contextualized theological concept of holistic ministry when she wrote, "Christ's method alone will give true success in reaching the people. The Saviour *mingled* with men as one who *desired* their good. He *showed* His sympathy for them, *ministered* to their needs, and won their confidence. Then He bade them, 'Follow Me.' "[2] Jesus mingled with people, identified their needs, met their needs, and developed a trust relationship. Through the trust relationship, He built a bridge of trust between the church and the communities and then said to the people, "Follow Me."

This is why the mission of the church is the responsibility of every person who believes in Him—to become a disciple and make disciples through personal engagement and relationship building. This means serving the whole person, a concept known as holistic ministry.

"Relationships are the method. Jesus invited people into relationships with himself; he loved them and in the process showed them how to follow God. His primary method was life-on-life."[3]

This is why the Savior *mingled* with men. The word *mingle* comes from *mignumi* (mig-noo-mee), a Greek word meaning to mix, surety, meddle, mingled, pledges, becomes, engaged, intermeddle, mortgaged, occupiers, occupy, or to undertake.

The following texts are examples where the word *mingled* is used to indicate different actions:

1. Luke 13:1: "There were present at that season some that told him of the Galilaeans, whose blood Pilate had *mingled* with their sacrifices" (KJV; emphasis added)—this implies "to mix, to mingle," chiefly diluting the wine so they blended and formed compound, as in wine and water.
2. Matthew 27:34: "They gave him vinegar to drink *mingled* with gall: and when he had tasted thereof, he would not drink" (KJV; emphasis added)—this implies a mixing without such composition, as in two sorts of grain.[4]
3. Revelation 14:10: "The same shall drink of the wine of the wrath of God, which is poured out without *mixture* into the cup of his indignation; and he shall be tormented with fire and brimstone in the presence of the holy angels, and in the presence of the Lamb" (KJV; emphasis added). In this text the word *mingled* or *mixture* is followed by *akratos*, meaning "unmixed, pure" (*a*, negative, and *kratos*, adjective, equals the verb *kerannumi*), which indicates that the two words used together form an oxymoron.

Jesus *mingled* with people, all creatures of God, including the disadvantaged and marginalized people of society. But He did not become part of the group in behavior, nor did He share common values or principles of life. Even though Jesus was in the midst of controversial groups of people that had been labeled as outcasts by the norm of society, He chose not to be part of their attitude, meddling with their customs and behaviors. Jesus maintained Christian values and biblical principles regardless of His encounters and circumstances and demonstrated the love of God while proclaiming the good news.

There are times we, as twenty-first-century Christians, do not want to mingle with people outside the walls of our church, nor outside our comfort zones. Throughout all levels of educational experiences we have not been inclusive of people who were not within our boundaries (i.e., family, school, church, job, etc.). Perhaps we were taught not to mingle with people of the world who are so-called sinners. That was definitely not the case with Jesus: He was among the people, people who were children of God, children who were created by God. In order to share the good news, we must mingle with people in our communities regardless of their socioeconomic status, race, gender, and so on.

When we mingle with people as Jesus did, we will truly be able to develop a new relationship with our communities. We will break down the barriers between church and community: spiritual, geographical, cultural, class, race, physical, and so forth. We will begin to welcome people—anyone who walks through the doors of our churches. We will begin to develop an efficient network within the community and cultivate a sense of belonging, interweaving the interests of the church and the community. When we take the church into the community, the community will accept the church, not as a social, religious assembly, but as one who has respect for the community and is able to embrace the differences.

He *desired* their good

The word *desired* comes from *epipotheo* (ep-ee-poth-eh'-o), a Greek word meaning to long for, desire, to pursue with love, to long after, to greatly desire, to earnestly desire.

The apostle Paul testifies of the will of our Savior in Romans 10:1: "Brothers and sisters, my heart's desire and prayer to God for the Israelites is that they may be saved." God wants His children to seek a covenant relationship with Him, to submit to God's righteousness. People are missing the fact that salvation comes through Christ Jesus. We seek our own righteousness and salvation through our works and efforts—salvation is relational. We are drawn by faith to Jesus Christ into communion with God the Father, and as a byproduct of this relationship, we establish a renewed relationship with the people around us. However, we often focus on internal issues (keeping the law, keeping the Sabbath, and earning own salvation), neglecting the millions of people who are in need of Jesus.

"Some men brought to him [Jesus] a paralyzed man, lying on a mat. When Jesus saw their faith, he said to the man, 'Take heart, son; your sins are forgiven' " (Matthew 9:2). People were brought before Jesus with physical, social, mental, and spiritual needs, and He desired their well-being as a whole person; not only were their physical needs met, but also their sins were forgiven. Jesus demonstrates that He has the ability to heal and the authority to forgive sins.

"Then Jesus asked them, 'Which is lawful on the Sabbath: to do good or to do evil, to save life or to kill?' But they remained silent" (Mark 3:4). The Pharisees acted as self-proclaimed religion police and accused Jesus of being a Sabbath violator. Jesus never refuted keeping the Sabbath holy; in fact, He simply affirms it by doing good. The question is not about whether we do activities on the Sabbath; doing good is always expected of Christians, regardless of the day of the week.

Jesus *desired* physical good for those with diseases, hunger, nakedness, no shelter; social good as He socialized with people who were outcasts from their society, the disenfranchised; mental good for those demon possessed, with their own religious preferences of understanding the intellectual concept; and spiritual good for those who were sincerely seeking the truth and had a longing for a Savior. "The King will reply, 'Truly I tell you, whatever you did for one of the least of these brothers and sisters of mine, you did for me' " (Matthew 25:40). Caring for the suffering and outcast is the duty of Christ's disciples.

Works of compassion do not secure salvation, but they do confirm that we belong to Christ and the kingdom of God. Jesus asks us how we have cared for the hungry, thirsty, strangers, naked, sick, and imprisoned in Matthew 25:31–46. It is about how we respond to His gospel, not what we do or do not do in our life—but if we follow Jesus. If we love God, it is inevitable that we will love His people. The apostle James said, "Pure and undefiled religion in the sight of our God and Father is this: to visit [have care for] orphans and widows in their distress, and to keep oneself unstained by the world" (James 1:27, NASB). To love others is compassion in action—not only family and friends, but people who are suffering, marginalized, and oppressed. In fact, the theological concept of holistic ministry is that when we care for others who are in need, we are actually caring for our Savior Jesus Christ.

He *showed* His sympathy for them

The word *mercy* comes from *eleeo* (el-eh-eh'-o), a Greek word meaning to have mercy on, to obtain mercy, show mercy, have compassion, have pity on, to help one afflicted or seeking aid, to bring help to the wretched, and to experience mercy.

The following texts illustrate where the word *showed* is used in multiple settings:

1. "Blessed are the merciful: for they shall obtain mercy" (Matthew 5:7, KJV). Christians must demonstrate forgiveness toward people who are dwelling in darkest guilt and sin, and show kindness to the hurting and needy. We should share Christ's compassionate mercy because we have *experienced* His mercy. Showing mercy is a heart attitude that opens a person to receive the offer of mercy from Jesus Christ.

2. "But I say unto you, Love your enemies, bless them that curse you, do good to them that hate you, and pray for them which despitefully use you, and persecute you; that ye may be the children of your Father which is in heaven: for he maketh his sun to rise on the evil and on the good, and sendeth rain on the just and on the unjust" (Matthew 5:44, 45, KJV). Jesus showed His sympathy for all people, not only family and friends but also enemies who had done injustice to Him and us. In fact, that is God's character. Christians are empowered to love and be sympathetic to people as Jesus was. Reaching out to people with the message of reconciliation between God and man also brings a reconciled relationship between others and us.

3. "Shouldn't you have had mercy on your fellow servant just as I had on you?" (Matthew 18:33). Jesus' teachings and standards created confusion within Judaism and the conventional culture and expectations—merciful, immeasurable forgiveness with unlimited grace. We can't understand His values all the time—we want justice. However, we also have learned and experienced in our own journey of inequity: grace does not keep count nor keep records. We must be irrational for God and His values.

4. "But love your enemies, do good to them, and lend to them without expecting to get anything back. Then your reward will be great, and you will be children of the Most High, because he is kind to the ungrateful and wicked. Be merciful, just as your Father is merciful" (Luke 6:35, 36). It is the golden rule of Christianity. It is not common sense, but it is God's character and His values. When we treat each other the way we would want to be treated, we naturally obey all the commands of God. In my humble opinion, when we return good with good, that is humanity; when we return good with evil, that is satanic; but, when we return evil with good—that is Christianity.

Jesus showed sympathy to people who were in need. In fact, Jesus came to earth from heaven to die for us, not because we deserved it, but because we needed His death to bring salvation to the world. Isaiah 53:5 says,

> But he was pierced for our transgressions,
>   he was crushed for our iniquities;
> the punishment that brought us peace was on him,
>   and by his wounds we are healed.

Christ demonstrated self-denial for the sake of sinners, people who are in need of salvation. Therefore, when we put others before and above us, we will begin to experience true life in Christianity.

He *ministered* to their needs

The word *ministered* comes from *diakoneo* (dee-ak-on-eh'-o), a Greek word meaning to be a servant, attendant, domestic, to serve, to wait at a table and offer food and drink to the guests, to minister (i.e., supply food and necessities of life, distribute the things necessary to sustain life).

In Matthew 20:28, Jesus clarifies His purpose: "Even as the Son of man came not to be ministered unto, but to minister, and to give his life a ransom for many" (KJV). Jesus took a servant-leadership role, a servant who is hired to maintain the master's will and serve others. So as Christians, we are called to serve the welfare of humanity and the church. We are commissioned to serve others and live a servant's life.

Also, in Luke 3:11 John the Baptist said, "Anyone who has two shirts should share with the one who has none, and anyone who has food should do the same." Jesus is not only concerned with our eternal salvation—meeting our spiritual needs—but He's also concerned with the daily aspects of our lives: sharing what we have with people who are in need, feeding the hungry, refusing to cheat or be unfair in business transactions, and making sure that we will not use our power to oppress the vulnerable.

In Matthew 6:2 we read, "So when you give to the needy, do not announce it with trumpets, as the hypocrites do in the synagogues and on the streets, to be honored by others. Truly I tell you, they have received their reward in full." Poverty was widespread in the first century, as it is today, and followers of Christ took seriously the obligation to provide for the needy. Jesus commands His disciples to practice generosity while being concerned about protecting both the dignity and the respect of the recipients who receive help. In Ezekiel 16:49, we read, "Now this was the sin of your sister Sodom: She and her daughters were arrogant, overfed and unconcerned; they did not help the poor and needy." But, there are times when we entertain ostensible motives in helping others and would like to obtain tangible benefits from the situation.

Putting all these attributes together, we see, as Jim Putman and Bobby Harrington put it,

that a disciple is a person who

1. is following Christ *(head)*;
2. is being changed by Christ *(heart)*;
3. is committed to the mission of Christ *(hands)*.[5]

Again, say Putman and Harrington,

we should ask the necessary head, heart, and hands questions that relate to this sphere.

1. *Head:* Does the person I am discipling know what the Bible teaches about the church and the importance of his or her relationships with other believers?
2. *Heart:* Are they growing in their love for others in the body of Christ?
3. *Hands:* Have they developed the relational skills they need in order to have healthy relationships with other believers? Are they using their gifts to minister to believers who are in need, or are they doubting and in need of encouragement? Is there a skill that I should teach them to help them grow in this sphere?[6]

Studying Jesus' method for making disciples and then studying how the early church repeated this pattern, we see a blueprint that we can follow as well. This simple blueprint is based on four words: share, connect, minister, and disciple.[7]

> "A disciple is a person who is following Christ *(head)*; is being changed by Christ *(heart)*; is committed to the mission of Christ *(hands)*."
> —Jim Putman

"Jesus **shared** who he was through words and deeds," Putman and Harrington write. "When people accepted his message, he invited them to **connect** with him in relationship. During that time of sharing life together, he taught them the truth about himself. As these disciples grew, Jesus trained them to **minister** to the lost and to his other followers. Finally, after Jesus rose from the dead, he deployed his followers to **disciple** others."[8]

Christ's methodology of reaching out to people was based on personal relationship development through sharing, connecting, ministering, and discipling others. It was holistic engagement and a strategy for drawing people closer to God. Our church has a long-standing tradition of providing lots of opportunities for our people to get involved; however, it is often event-driven rather than applying the true essence of Christ's methodology in educating and equipping disciples.

Christ's methodology was personal relationship building: sharing the good news and sharing the love of God, connecting people to God through evangelism and worship, connecting people through community and discipleship, connecting people to the city through mercy and justice, connecting people to the culture through the integration of faith and work, ministering holistically, ministering for the betterment of life—physically, mentally, socially, and spiritually—and making disciples. Through life-on-life evangelism, we are building a trust relationship.

Unfortunately, instead of investing our time and effort in building a relationship, we often expect certain behaviors to be demonstrated immediately, especially from the newly baptized members of the church. Based on superficial and external behaviors, we tend to make a judgment call on their beliefs. If we see the expected behavior, we say that he or she has the right spirit; but if they don't deliver the expected changes, we say that they don't have the Holy Spirit. We are convinced that right beliefs will produce the right behaviors.

However, we live in a VUCA world (V-volatility, U-uncertainty, C-complexity, and A-ambiguity).[9] And each person's worldview is developed based on his or her VUCA environments, such as culture, custom, values, principles, education, socioeconomic views, political views, and so forth. Furthermore, faith is processed through the VUCA worldview, and our behaviors are formulated and developed. The VUCA worldview is the filter system through which institutional beliefs are learned, analyzed, and processed, and then the behavior is determined.

Our focus should not be on the end product—the behaviors only. We should focus on their VUCA environments, their journey, and their lives—how they lived their lives. When we understand a person's life, we can understand why such behaviors exist. When we understand the person's journey, we can minister to them with relevant and effective holistic ministries. Christ's methodology was holistic engagement for the well-being of the whole person: physically, socially, mentally, and spiritually.

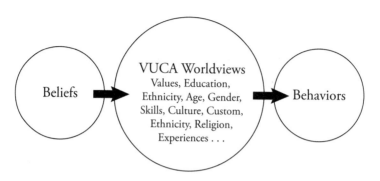

Holistic concept

The word *holistic* comes from the Greek word *holos* (all, entire, total), which implies that all aspects of human life (biological, chemical, social, economic, mental, spiritual, etc.) cannot be determined or explained by the sum of its component parts alone.[10] It also takes into account the root word *shalom* (peace, well-being, welfare, prosperity, safety, health, perfect, whole, full, just), indicating that God wants us to have a complete and full life. In fact, it is the most important covenant that God made with His children, and keeping the covenant relationship is our duty and responsibility as Christians—not only to God, but also to others.[11]

Holos is also the same root word for abundant life, fullness of life, and a perfect life. So when Jesus said, "You ought to have a perfect life, as your Father in heaven," He didn't mean you have to develop an unblemished character, or be a sinless person; He meant we need to be perfect as *holos*; we need to have a well-being of life: physical, social, mental, and spiritual.

Perhaps this is why Jewish people greet each other by saying, "Shalom." To me, they are saying: *Are you well? Are you peaceful? Are you having an abundant life? Do you have the fullness of life? Are you being perfect physically, socially, mentally, and spiritually?*

When we engage with people, we can't say, "I don't care about you, as long as I'm a perfect Christian," or "I don't care what you do with your body, as long as you study the Bible and become a church member." When we approach people, we need to say, "Brother, I'm concerned about you—your whole person being well. I'm praying for you." We need to be concerned about people as whole persons: their physical, social, mental, and spiritual well-being. This is the foundation of holistic ministry. And this is the way Jesus approached people.

The purpose of holistic ministry is not only to proclaim the good news, the word of salvation, but also to demonstrate the love of God to people who are in need. It is a balanced outreach that proclaims the gospel as well as demonstrates God's love and concern for every soul. It is seeing and ministering to the whole person.

That's how we love people in Jesus' name. We need to break the barrier between the church and the community. We've created a fortress around the church and have taken an attitude such as, "We're holy and good, and you're unholy and sinful," and we need to break it down. We need to practice what we preach; holistic ministry focuses on personal and spiritual transformation.

Sometimes we just like to convict people of their wrong behavior, and we hope that somehow we'll convert them—which is just transferring information from head to head. But holistic engagement isn't just transferring head knowledge from one head to another; it is speaking from your heart and connecting people in a heart-to-heart way. When we are connected heart to heart, we will create a trust relationship between individuals and we will earn the right and privilege to share the truth that we have.

The Christian experience and holistic ministry is more important than ever before, especially in the twenty-first century. In my perspective, the following are typical traditional evangelism strategies:

1. Churches engage with cognitive disquisition and confront others over biblical findings; speaking through the logical mind-set to prove the Bible speaks the truth.
2. By convicting people that they are wrong, then people will be converted; through the conversion experience, behaviors will be changed.
3. The converted will be welcomed by demonstrating the expected external, superficial behaviors.

However, most people are committing their lives to Christ through friendship—personal relationships, and by mingling and developing trusted relationship. Christians begin to influence non-Christian values and principles of life, and as a consequence, people develop a stronger commitment and accept Jesus not only as their Savior, but as Lord of their lives. Life-on-life relationship building is the key method.

This is why we witness about Jesus and see Him as the model example of the holistic approach. He has dealt with each one of us as a whole person, because we were created in the same manner. Ellen White says in her book *Education*, "When Adam came from the Creator's hand, he bore, in his *physical, mental, and spiritual nature, a likeness to his Maker.* 'God created man in His own image,' and it was His purpose that the longer man lived, the more fully he should reveal this image,— the more fully reflect the glory of the Creator. All his faculties were capable of development; their capacity and vigor were continually to increase."[12]

Throughout Jesus' ministry, we witness a genuine holistic approach toward humanity, especially people who are marginalized and disadvantaged. The poor, the sick, the unclean, the prostitutes, and tax collectors, they were all outcasts and sinful people. Jesus expanded the kingdom of God to places, people, and cultures that the Jews had never considered God to be interested in. In fact, He was the fulfillment of the Messianic job description found in Isaiah 61.

Isaiah 61 indicates the means by which God's people can be enabled to live righteous lives, which will in turn draw all nations to God through the Anointed One, the Messiah. Verses 1–7 present the benefits that the Messiah's people will receive. In verses 8 and 9, God makes explicit His desires for covenant righteousness and that He alone makes that righteousness possible. In verses 10 and 11, the servant people break into a psalm of praise to God, who makes them a righteous people in the sight of the nations.

According to Matthew 11:2–6, when John the Baptist was being held in prison and began to doubt his convictions that Jesus was the Christ, the Anointed One, the Messiah, John sent two of his disciples to Jesus to ask, "Are you the one who is to come, or should we expect someone else?" (v. 3). Jesus replied, "Go back and report to John what you hear and see: The blind receive sight, the lame walk, those who have leprosy are cleansed, the deaf hear, the dead are raised, and the good news is proclaimed to the poor. Blessed is anyone who does not stumble on account of me" (vv. 4–6).

Jesus was simply reminding them of the Messianic job description in Isaiah 61 and readdressed the Messianic kingdom in a different way than John the Baptist and his disciples had expected. Rather than overthrowing the Roman Empire, each blind, outcast, sick, or enslaved person experienced the life-transforming good news of the gospel. For Jesus, making a difference in the lives of people was part of His work as the Messiah.

Jesus' calling

In Matthew 9:35, "Jesus went through all the towns and villages, teaching in their synagogues, proclaiming the good news of the kingdom and healing every disease and sickness." Here, Jesus mingles with people by visiting the towns and villages where the people are, teaching the good news, and healing people who are in need. He grieved over the multitudes of people who were helpless, and He brought hope to their lives by ministering to their needs. Through this compassionate service opportunity, Jesus was able to build a trust relationship.

For example, Jesus healed all diseases (Matthew 4:23), the centurion's servant (8:5–13), the blind and dumb demoniac (12:22), the sick by the touch of His garment (14:34–36), the daughter of the woman of Canaan (15:21–28), the epileptic (17:14–21), one who had an unclean spirit (Mark 1:21–28), a paralytic (2:1–5), a demon-possessed man (5:1–20), and so on.

Moreover, Jesus exemplifies the holistic ministry through His own incarnation. God became one of us. The Creator became a creation. Jesus didn't send a messenger, didn't just reach out a hand to pull us up, but Jesus Himself came. He became like one of us and lived among us.

However, because of this very act of commitment by our God, who became incarnated and lived among us, we killed Jesus. "We killed Jesus, not because he claimed to be the Messiah but because he became like us. That is a blasphemy against our greatest hopes for what a messiah will do. We don't want a savior who descends into our humanity. We want a savior who will rescue us from all the judgments we have faced."[13]

Jesus' commission

Jesus commands the Great Commission in Matthew 28:20, "[Teach] them to observe all things whatsoever I have commanded you: and, lo, I am with you always, even unto the end of the world" (KJV). Jesus commands us to teach to others all things that He has commanded to us. What are His commands?

- *Come to Me*, especially all who are heavy laden (11:28). As people in need, regardless of whether it's physical, social, mental, or spiritual, we must come to Jesus in daily life devotion. He promises forgiveness, hope, and assurance of salvation.
- *Learn of Me*. Jesus proclaims, "I am meek and lowly in heart: and ye shall find rest unto your souls" (11:29, KJV). This

command indicates building a relationship between God and His people—knowing God, being connected with Him, not just worshiping God out of fear of punishment. John Milton said, "The end of all learning is to know God, and out of that knowledge to love and imitate Him."[14] It is to know God, not just know about God and people.

- *Believe in Me.* Jesus speaks on several occasions that He is God (John 14:1, 11; 17:21; etc.) and we must believe. People throughout human history continually seek God; however, many create their own philosophy of life without finding God the Creator, Redeemer, and Judge. It is the duty of Christians to bring souls to Christ, inviting them to be part of the kingdom of heaven.

- *Follow Me.* It is the greatest calling of all. It is an honor and privilege to be part of God's mission—to do His purpose. But the cost of discipleship seems too great to bear for some, so many leave Jesus to follow their own will, life ambitions, or desires for self-fulfillment. John MacArthur said, "The Christian life is not adding Jesus to one's own way of life but renouncing that personal way of life for His and being willing to pay whatever cost that may require."[15] People come to Jesus willing to accept Him as Savior of their lives but meet challenges in accepting Him as the *Lord* of their lives. Self-denial and self-sacrificing love is not as easy as it seems. "By this we know love, that he [Jesus] laid down his life for us, and we ought to lay down our lives for the brothers. But if anyone has the world's goods and sees his brother in need, yet closes his heart against him, how does God's love abide in him? Little children, let us not love in word or talk but in deed and in truth. By this we shall know that we are of the truth and reassure our heart before him" (1 John 3:16–19, ESV). When we follow Jesus, others will see to whom we belong.

- *Abide in Me.* As God lives in us by the Holy Spirit, we must live in Him. As God the Creator, He is above us; as God the Redeemer, He is with us as Immanuel; and as God the Judge, He is in us as the Holy Spirit. In Galatians 2:20 we read, "I have been crucified with Christ, so it is no longer I who am living, but it is Christ who is living in me; and the life I am now living in the flesh, I am living in faith of the Son of God who loved me and gave himself up for me" (Montgomery).

We must dwell in His will and follow His commands, teaching others to obey everything that Jesus commanded us. This is a biblical mandate for His disciples as we share Christ's love with the community. Through consistent community outreach ministries, we begin to knock down the barriers between churches and their communities. Through faith in action, Christians demonstrate servant leadership. We are to work for change in societal injustices that bring discrimination against race, gender, age, socioeconomic status, and so forth. By Christ's model of compassionate service and love, we could lead people to spiritual transformation.

According to Ronald Sider, Philip Olson, and Heidi Rolland Unruh, the holistic ministry is a door to a trusted relationship in relief operations, individual and community development, and structural changes: *relief* involves directly supplying food, clothing, or housing to someone in urgent need—it is simply *to give a hungry person a fish*. *Individual development* includes transformational ministries that empower a person to improve his or her physical, emotional, intellectual, relational, or social status—it is to *teach a person to fish*. *Community development* renews the building blocks of a healthy community, such as housing, jobs, health care, and education—*to provide a person fishing equipment*. *Structural change* means transforming unfair political, economic, environmental, or cultural institutions and systems. It is to make sure that everyone in the community has equal opportunity by *helping everybody get fair access to the fish pond*.[16]

Here are some samples of social ministry types presented by Sider, Olson, and Unruh:[17]

Social Ministry—Housing	
Relief	Homeless shelter, emergency housing
Individual Development	Home-ownership seminar, credit counseling
Community Development	Affordable housing construction and rehabilitation
Structural Change	Lobbying against redlining and other unfair lending practices, suing slumlords to improve housing conditions

Social Ministry—*Un*employment and *Under*employment	
Relief	Food pantry, clothes closet
Individual Development	GED tutoring, job training, budget counseling
Community Development	Day care center and after-school program for children of working parents, training in small business start-up
Structural Change	Advocating to raise the minimum wage and Earned Income Tax Credit, promoting tax incentives for job creation in low-income areas

Social Ministry—Family Brokenness	
Relief	Family crisis hotline, family services information, referral clearinghouse
Individual Development	Parenting classes, family counseling, divorce-recovery support group
Community Development	Legal-aid clinic that offers family services, family mediation court
Structural Change	Encouraging employers to adopt family-friendly policies, promoting pro-marriage legislation

Social Ministry—Health	
Relief	Free immunizations, vouchers for medicines
Individual Development	Overeaters Anonymous support group, health seminars
Community Development	Community gymnasium, health clinic with sliding scale fees
Structural Change	Lobbying for affordable health insurance, antismoking campaigns

Through holistic ministry, we give people new hope, motivation, dignity, and self-esteem. Through the holistic community outreach ministries, we could heal the scars from past negative experiences and relationships. We need to pray for God's intervention in the holistic ministry that we are planning for our communities, listen to God's guidance, listen to the challenges of the people in our communities, and look for an opportunity to serve and connect. By doing so, we will truly experience the genuine fellowship that currently exists in the kingdom of God.

Tony Campolo, professor emeritus of sociology at Eastern University, said, "This new world the prophet [Isaiah] envisioned is a world God is even now initiating through those who are willing to follow the Spirit's leading in transforming the world that is. Christians are increasingly catching this vision and promoting God's holistic salvation that not only provides eternal life but also challenges all God's people to love the oppressed and look for justice in this present age."[18]

> "This new world the prophet [Isaiah] envisioned is a world God is even now initiating through those who are willing to follow the Spirit's leading in transforming the world that is. Christians are increasingly catching this vision and promoting God's holistic salvation that not only provides eternal life but also challenges all God's people to love the oppressed and look for justice in this present age."
> —Tony Campolo

Why do we cry for worldly wealth? Why do we seek after honors and praise of the world? Why do we rush after immediate gratification, temporary pleasure? Why this eager search for wisdom outside the will of God? Jesus said to the Samaritan woman, "But whoever drinks the water I give them will never thirst. Indeed, the water I give them will become in them a spring of water welling up to eternal life" (John 4:14). But, instead of seeking the water from God, we yearn for material possessions and societal status. Where is our compassion to end poverty? Where is our vision to stop world hunger? Where is our mission to stop human trafficking? Where is our desire to build a happy home? Where is our commitment for a life of integrity and humility and peace? Are we just craving financial success, external beauty, and getting ahead at work?

Because of personal ambition, some of us become religious practitioners, Christians without Christ. We go to church systematically and mechanically, week after week, and participate in a religious ritual.

We see people in need everywhere, but the challenge is that we don't see God's people. We see stereotypes, causes, and external appearances—we don't see people who have the same need for God. We need to pray for God's vision in our lives, to see His people through His eyes. To see people, with faces in the image of God.

Sider, Olson, and Unruh said that service ministry (servant evangelism) is the door to evangelism, focusing on

- ministries of personal spiritual transformation as a path to social change;
- social services ministries as a door to evangelism;
- ministries of reconciliation that witness to unity in Christ;
- community development to express God's love for whole persons and communities;
- justice ministries that embody the empowering message of the gospel; and
- reaching skeptics by demonstrating that the church makes a difference.[19]

The apostle John says, "That which was from the beginning, which we have heard, which we have seen with our eyes, which we have looked at and our hands have touched—this we proclaim concerning the Word of life. The life appeared; we have seen it and testify to it, and we proclaim to you the eternal life, which was with the Father and has appeared to us" (1 John 1:1, 2). Christianity is not just a conceptual framework that we study and discuss. It's not just engaging cognitive disquisition about who's right and wrong. Christianity has to be tangible—something that people can touch, feel, and smell through our individual lives and collectively through our church. It has to be real. But we love *talking* about Christianity, yet we *don't demonstrate* it in our lives.

Ellen White emphasized the importance of holistic ministry when she wrote, "Christ's method alone will give true success in reaching the people. The Saviour *mingled* with men as one who *desired* their good. He *showed* His sympathy for them, *ministered* to their needs, and won their confidence. Then He bade them, 'Follow Me.' "[20]

At each component, Christ's method of social dimensions of evangelism could be defined. You can't just go into "Follow Me" mode; it's a journey. You have to mingle, have the desire for their good, show sympathy, minister, win their confidence—then you have the right to say, "Follow Me." Christ's methodology was based on relationship-building environments, and His focus was discipleship.

Relationships are the method. Jesus dealt with the whole person, not only the spiritual aspect of human life—He understood the physical, social, and mental aspects of the human being. His ministry was not just focused on organized religious institutions' membership increase, but to make the world a better place to live and prepare for eternal life. In my humble opinion, He was not only our Savior, but also a social entrepreneur as indicated throughout the Gospels. Jesus and His disciples were focusing on holistic ministry. They implemented ministries, and as a byproduct of these ministries, organized congregations were developed. The purpose of the church is not to be a social club, but a lighthouse to bring people to Jesus and to build the kingdom of God.

I grew up in South Korea, and there are rice fields everywhere. Let's say I'm standing in the corner of a rice field, holding an empty bag, and I say, "God, I know You'll bless me and fill my bag with rice, because I'm faithful." But the problem is that I don't step into the rice field. I don't cultivate the field, don't fertilize it, irrigate it—I don't do anything. I don't invest any time and resources, no sweat equity into the rice field throughout the whole year. But I show up with an empty bag once a year and tell God to fill the bag with rice. Does that make sense? No farming, no harvest. How can you have harvest without farming?

Now look at our church behavior. That's exactly what we do. We don't invest our time and resources into farming, but we want the harvest. That mind-set has to change.

I went to a certain church, and they had their core values hanging in their foyer. It said, "Personal Salvation, Spiritual Discipline, Seeking the Lord in Worship, and Becoming a devoted follower." The pastor asked me, "What do you think about our core values? We worked hard for the last six months coming up with these wonderful values for this church."

It was nice, but I actually had a problem with these values. My mother's family is Buddhist; my wife's family is Buddhist. I grew up with Buddhism, and if we change a word, "Seeking the Lord" to "Seeking Buddha," in my humble opinion, it's the essence of Buddhism. It's all about MY salvation. It's about the private atonement gospel, self-serving Christianity. There's nothing about other people, just ME on that list.

Christianity isn't about me, but about God and His people—not just on the inside, but also outside the walls of the church. But those values in the church were talking about what I can get out of Christianity. Churches need to become missional churches, not attractional churches. No more "Come and see"; rather, we must "Go" where people are.

This is why Jesus called out to them, "Come, follow me, and I will show you how to fish for people!" (Matthew 4:19, NLT). If you read Matthew 4 in the King James Version, it says, "I will make you fishers of men." Often the evangelical community uses this passage as a salesmanship tool. "I'm going to teach you how to give a Bible study so you can win souls and become the number one salesperson of our denomination." That's the typical interpretation of this beautiful passage.

But when you read this text in the holistic community outreach ministry perspective, it says, "I will teach you how to fish *for the people*." The focus is the people, not us gaining a skillset. It's about teaching us, so we can do something for the people—it's about serving people.

Let me expand on that. Imagine I'm a fisherman, and I would bring fish to the market so people would buy from me. Affluent community people, who have the means, will come to this market and buy fish. And on the side of the stall, I'll have a basket of fish that isn't marketable—the heads are crushed, the sides are open, and so forth, and people in an affluent community won't buy these defective and unappealing fish. But as a Christian, I've set aside these undesirable fish for those considered "the least of these"—the orphans, widows, lepers, Samaritans, prostitutes, or Gentiles: the ones who can't afford the regular price, or couldn't shop at the regular market, so they come after hours to access my unsold fish.

This is why Jesus tells us that He will *teach us* how to fish (to take care of) ALL the people in our community—the affluent community, and especially the "least of these." The least, last, and lost, who are disenfranchised, disconnected, disassociated, or excommunicated from our families, neighbors, and communities. They are our obligation. When we reach out to the community, it's not just the physical needs of people that we need to address, but also the well-being of the whole person.

Yes, some people are in need of provisional services such as food and clothes, but there are others in the community who want to contribute and participate in good ministries. People who are in the fifth category of self-actualization want to contribute to the needs of their society. They are seeking opportunities to be involved, engaged, and make a difference. So we have to create an opportunity for them to engage and serve. Community outreach is not just about giving out food and clothing once a year, and getting satisfaction doing it. It's about connecting with other people, and connecting God with His people. We have to look at the entire spectrum of Maslow's hierarchy and try to develop the ministry around the needs.

To apply the principle of Maslow's hierarchy of needs, we must pray to God for His intervention in our lives, listen to people's struggles and challenges, and look for an opportunity to serve and demonstrate the love of God. When we intentionally and sincerely approach people who are affluent, disenfranchised, disassociated, and marginalized in our communities, we will begin to witness and influence people's lives and transform our communities for the kingdom of God on earth, as it is in heaven.

As Bible-believing Christians, we often contemplate that we have the truth, but we have not earned the right to share the truth, nor have we earned the trust of our community. People need not only to hear the good news, but to see Jesus through the lives of His disciples. Just as God came down from heaven to the world, we must go out into the world to reach people where they are. We are instruments of God's will, and that is our calling; it is our mission—the reason for our existence.

We should not just focus on successful ministry through quantitative growth, such as church membership expansion, institutional expansion, or financial increases, but concentrate on the outcome of individual lives—make a difference in a person's life and how we can benefit our community. *Is our community a better place to live because we as Christians invested our lives for others? Have we made a sustainable impact in our communities through our faithful presence?*

Holistic ministry is about being faithful to our Savior and Lord Jesus Christ for His calling, commission, and commandment. When we are faithful, we will have successful outcomes. When we walk with Jesus in a faithful journey, we will grow in His light and His will.

Let us pray for *Shalom*!

---

1. Jim Putman and Bobby Harrington with Robert E. Coleman, *DiscipleShift: Five Steps That Help Your Church to Make Disciples Who Make Disciples*, Exponential Series (Grand Rapids, MI: Zondervan, 2013), 25–28.

2. White, *Ministry of Healing*, 143; emphasis added.

3. Putman and Harrinton, *DiscipleShift*, 33.

4. H. G. Liddell and R. Scott, Henry Stuart Jones, Roderick McKenzie, *A Greek-English Lexicon* (Oxford: Clarendon Press, 1940).

5. Putman and Harrington, *DiscipleShift*, 51; italics in the original.

6. Putman and Harrinton, *DiscipleShift*, 87.

7. Putman and Harrinton, *DiscipleShift*, 153.

8. Putman and Harrinton, *DiscipleShift*, 153

9. Paul Kinsinger and Karen Walch, "Living and Leading in a VUCA World" (Thunderbird University, 2012).

10. Henry George Liddell, Robert Scott, *An Intermediate Greek-English Lexicon: Founded Upon the Seventh Edition of Liddell and Scott's Greek-English Lexicon* (Clarendon Press, 1968).

11. Mark I. Wallace, "The Spirit of Environmental Justice: Resurrection Hope in Urban America," *Worldviews: Global Religions, Culture, and Ecology* 12, no. 2 (2008): 255–269.

12. Ellen G. White, *Education* (Oakland, CA: Pacific Press®, 1903), 15; emphasis added. The scripture quoted within this quote is from Genesis 1:27 (see KJV).

13. Barnes, *When God Interrupts*, Kindle edition, chap. 4.

14. John Milton, http://www.azquotes.com/quote/362802.

15. MacArthur, *Matthew 8-15*, The MacArthur New Testament Commentary, 24.

16. Sider, Olson, and Unruh, *Churches That Make a Difference*, 86.

17. Sider, Olson, and Unruh, *Churches That Make a Difference*, 86, 87.

18. Tony Campolo,

19. Sider, Olson, and Unruh, *Churches That Make a Difference*, 35–44.

20. White, *Ministry of Healing*, 143; emphasis added.

PART II:

WHAT—What Are the Components to Revisit and Reframe?

CHAPTER 3

The Missional Church Movement

One day I took my family to a park where a river runs nearby. As I knelt on the banks of the river, I saw a huge decorative box floating down with the river's current. At the same moment, I noticed a small fish right below my knees, swimming against the river's current. Two objects passing in opposite directions—one going down with the river's current, the other going against it. There were many differences, but the biggest difference was life.

The box was humongous, well-decorated, and impressive looking, but because it had no life, it was going along with the river's current. But the fish, so small and insignificant that it wouldn't even be enough for sushi or a tuna sandwich, had life, and it was swimming against the river's current.

As a church, if we do not have a clearly defined mission or understand the purpose of our existence, we are no different than that box. David J. Bosch said, "Mission is not primarily an activity of the church, but an attribute of God. God is a missionary God. . . . Mission is thereby seen as a movement from God to the world; the church is viewed as an instrument for that mission. There is church because there is mission, not vice versa. To participate in mission is to participate in the movement of God's love toward people, since God is a fountain of sending love."[1]

This is why we must follow God's inspiration and instruction: to have a plan and make the journey. We must mingle with the people, have a desire for their holistic well-being, demonstrate sympathy, and minister to their needs. Then we will have the confidence and the right to share the good news.

The purpose of the church is to reach our community for the glory of our Lord. The church exists for this missional purpose. Therefore, we must invest our time, energy, and resources to enlighten, educate, develop, and equip disciples who will join with us in this missional movement; and then these committed disciples will empower and make other disciples. This is the greatest movement of our God. God does not merely send the church on this mission. God already is in this mission, and He is inviting us to join Him.

God didn't call us just to be blessed; God is also sending us to be a blessing to others. Christianity is not about us coming to church once a week, having our emotional needs met, and then going home and repeating this pattern again and again. Christians cannot be just internally focused spiritual consumers. We are blessed; therefore, we must be a blessing to others.

> "I am of the opinion that my life belongs to the community, and as long as I live, it is my privilege to do for it whatever I can. I want to be thoroughly used up when I die, for the harder I work, the more I live."
> —George B. Shaw

George Bernard Shaw said, "I am of the opinion that my life belongs to the community, and as long as I live, it is my privilege to do for it whatever I can. I want to be thoroughly used up when I die, for the harder I work, the more I live."[2] As a missional church, we must enlighten, educate, develop, and equip people to be involved individually, and collectively as a church body. We cannot compromise to be an attractional church.

That's why Jesus said, "For even the Son of Man came not to be served but to serve others and to give his life as a ransom for many" (Matthew 20:28, NLT). Ellen White wrote, "The church is God's appointed agency for the salvation of men. It was organized for service, and its mission is to carry the gospel to the world."[3] That is why God inspired us with three essential functions of the church to complete its mission: discipleship, world mission, and community transformation.

Our mission cannot go forward without every member being involved, not only in telling people about the good news but also in service to the community and engaged in social justice. The true witness of Christians must be in both word and deed.

The mission of the church begins with God, who has a committed missional heart for the world that He created. The church is an expression of God's missional heart on this earth. When we become a missional church, then the church will become the hope of the world. Through this missional movement, we proclaim the good news of salvation, our Christ Jesus, and we demonstrate the love of God through our compassionate holistic community engagement. Whether we are young or old, whether we are male or female—it doesn't make any difference. We serve God and His people in a missional church; this is what we signed up for. We need to take the current passivity out of the church and be engaged proactively with our communities.

Alan Kreider said, "People were fascinated by it [Christianity], drawn to it as to a magnet."[4] Keller says Kreider "goes on to make a strong historical case that Christians' *lives*—their concern for the weak and the poor, their integrity in the face of persecution, their economic sharing, their sacrificial love even for their enemies, and the high quality of their common life together—attracted nonbelievers to the gospel."[5]

"Kreider observes that early Christianity grew explosively—40 percent per decade for nearly three centuries—in a very hostile environment," writes Keller.[6] Why is this not the reality today? It is because of our Pharisaical attitude regarding our theology: I am right—therefore, you must be wrong. I have an atheist friend who challenges my theology and does not respect my Christian values. However, he may be a better father to his children and husband to his wife than I have ever been to mine.

> "People were fascinated by it [Christianity], drawn to it as to a magnet."
> —Alan Kreider

In 1 John 1:1, 2 we read, "That which was from the beginning, which we have heard, which we have seen with our eyes, which we have looked at and our hands have touched—this we proclaim concerning the Word of life. The life appeared; we have seen it and testify to it, and we proclaim to you the eternal life, which was with the Father and has appeared to us." People must hear, see, and touch Christianity as something tangible through our lives. Mahatma Gandhi said, "I like your Christ, I do not like your Christians. Your Christians are so unlike your Christ."[7]

Jesus focused on discipleship, and His method was relationship development. Therefore, we must become relationship-developing churches. We must become a missional church. We must create relational environments, and eventually, with the Spirit's presence, people will mature spiritually.

As we encounter people in our daily life, we should engage them with genuine concern for their holistic well-being and share the good news, connecting them to God and ministering to their needs, and then we will begin to experience the presence of the Holy Spirit among us.

Read the story of the woman at the well in John 4. Look at verse 14. Jesus says to the woman, "But whoever drinks the water I give them will never thirst. Indeed, the water I give them will become in them a spring of water welling up to eternal life." But instead of seeking for the water from God, we desire material possessions and social status. *Where is our compassion to end poverty? Where is our vision to stop world hunger? Where is our mission to stop human trafficking? Where is our desire to build a happy home? Where is our commitment for a life of integrity and humility and peace? Or are we just craving financial success, external beauty, and getting ahead at work?*

There are challenges when we plan a community outreach ministry because we don't understand the community. We need to be more educated about the community and the environment—where our church is located.

To answer the above questions, we need to study the current trends and thoughts of our changing community, and why these demands are inevitable. When we develop broader comprehension of societal changes, we can develop relevant strategies to be more effective in operations and ministries.

Gerontologist Vern Bengtson contextualizes key factors of organizational operations and human behaviors throughout the development of aging theories of society in agriculture, industrial/technology, and globalization.[8] Stephen Covey, in his remarkable book *The 8th Habit*, contextualizes civilizations in five developments: first, the hunter/gatherer; second, the agricultural; third, the industrial; fourth, the information and knowledge worker; and fifth, "an emerging Age of Wisdom."[9] In the twenty-first century, I would call the fifth development the age of conceptualization.[10]

The key factors of each society uniquely characterize its attributes: at the beginning of our agricultural society the term *coordination* is a key factor; in industrial/technology, it is *cooperation*; in the age of globalization, it is *communication*; and in the age of conceptualization, *collaboration* becomes a mode of operation. Daniel H. Pink introduces and explains six key components and senses of the "conceptual age" as follows:[11]

1. Design—Moving beyond function to engage the senses
2. Story—Narrative added to products and services, not just argument

3. Symphony—Adding invention and big-picture thinking (not just detail focus)
4. Empathy—Going beyond logic and engaging emotion and intuition
5. Play—Bringing humor and lightheartedness to business and products
6. Meaning—Immaterial feelings and values of products.

We are living in an age of conceptualization,[12] heavily influenced by postmodernism and post-Christendom. In this age we focus on collaboration. People use these words, *cooperation* and *collaboration*, interchangeably, but there is a huge difference in the philosophical conceptual frameworks.

The difference between *cooperation* and *collaboration* can be perceived as contradictory in the industrial society and the conceptual society. The traditional definition of *cooperation*, according to the *World English Dictionary*, is, "Working together: the act of working or acting together to achieve a common goal," and "compliance: help provided by doing what is asked or required." *Collaboration* means "the act of working together with one or more people in order to achieve something."

In the conceptual age, one might see *cooperation* in the industrial age with negative connotations. The industrial age sustains its development based on hierarchical, bureaucratic organizational structure, even though its structure is functional and clearly defines each entity's role and responsibilities. The industrial/technology age ushered in a period in history characterized chiefly by the replacement of hand tools with power-driven machines. This, in turn, resulted in concentrations of industry in large bureaucratic and hierarchical establishments. Its organizational structure is based on positional authority and is leader-centric. The negative by-product of this organizational structure is that isolated "silos" are created at each organizational level that "cooperate" and co-exist independently from each other.

Cooperation is claiming pie pieces and forbidding anyone to take it. We draw lines between departments and ministries, and coexist/cooperate, but we do not share resources and manpower, trying to sustain ministry within departmental boundary. This is one of the reasons why churches are not effective in working internally with various church ministries and externally with public entities. We should be intentionally engaged in collaboration mode, where each entity shares resources and manpower to enhance organizational capacity and create greater benefits collectively and corporately.

Society expects *unity of efforts* through mission and vision, instead of *uniformity of command* through policies and procedures. In general, people are not interested in organized religious affiliations. So then, how do we reach them? The church must be relevant and able to contextualize the ministry.

What is contextualization? A social, ethnic, or cultural setting is a context. Each cultural or ethnic context is unique, growing out of unique worldview assumptions, which result in specific ways of thinking about and living life.[13] We should consider following six crucial components of contextualized ministry:

1. Diversified ministries: should expand the ministry portfolio beyond the walls of the church. Instead of a church program that is inward focused, we must be an outwardly focused church and provide relevant ministries.

2. Heart faith: instead of engaging in a logical, cognitive converting process of traditional proselytizing strategies in head-to-head information transitions, we must share life-changing stories of individuals from heart to heart on how God made a difference in their lives.

3. Change agents: engaging in dialogue with societal challenges and providing relevant community outreach ministries to equip individuals and develop community as a crucial aspect of being a Christian. The church should consider ministries such as English as a Second Language (ESL) and General Educational Development (GED) high school equivalency classes, after-school tutoring programs, community picnics, cultural difference discussion groups, and so forth.

4. Holistic ministry: Jesus not only taught people about salvation from sin; He took an interest in the whole person—physical, social, emotional, and spiritual. Ministering to people's needs could be expensive and time consuming, but it is our duty as Christians.

5. Excitement: vibrant ministry generates enthusiasm and promotes self-motivated commitment to the cause of its action. Through the enrichment of life experiences, one could shift from being a religious practitioner to experiencing a genuine fellowship with God in an intimate relationship.

6. Passing the legacy: through the faithful journey with Jesus Christ, we could transform the world into a better place to live and make a difference as a result of people's behavioral change. Because of

our churches, hospitals, and educational institutions, transformation is evident in communities, and we should pass on to our children the values of the kingdom of heaven.

After all, the Father has sent the Son, and the Son sends us (His disciples) into the world. "God's missional heart is what [motivated Him] to send Jesus into the world; the church is first and foremost an expression of God's missional heart. . . . The church's entire reason for existence is to be a faithful expression of God's missional purpose."[14] The ultimate job of a leader is to motivate people to accomplish this mission. When people are excited about what they do, they participate.

Postmodernism and post-Christendom heavily influence the conceptualization age, which states that thinking, feeling, empathy, authenticity, and finding meaning are all relevant and important to people. The story is just as important as the product or service. People desire whole community engagement with public, private, religious, and nongovernmental organization (NGO) sectors working together in a win-win relationship. These partnerships are effective in facilitating real change.

There actually is a great demand for churches in our society. People need churches to provide services for the community. So a church should provide diverse ministry opportunities: relief, individual and community development, and structured change/reform. One size doesn't fit all. A church doesn't only have to be provisional. A church should provide diversified opportunities for the people to be engaged and involved. Residents of affluent communities can come to your church, participate in the service, and contribute to others' needs.

Also, don't just talk about numbers and figures—tell the stories. *How has Jesus made a difference in your personal life and your community, through your church?* If you don't have a story to tell, people aren't interested in what you're offering. *Are you really the salt and the light of your own community? Do you have empathy? Do you cry with them? Do you rejoice with the people in your community?*

Some Christians say they are joyful. But when you go to church, do you see happy people? You go to church on Sabbath, and people say, "Happy Sabbath." Yet some people look grumpy, sorrowful, depressed. I hear "Happy Sabbath," but I don't feel happiness exuding from their hearts.

Christianity is exciting. When you wake up in the morning, are you excited? Do you wake up saying, "Thank You, Lord, for another day"?

Do you look forward to making a difference in this world? Are you excited about meeting people and touching lives? Or do you think and say, "Oh Lord, another day." Whatever we do as a church should not be a momentary program, only for the now.

We also need to include the children, youth, and young adults in the endeavors we are dreaming, so they can continue this journey. Dreams are something we cannot accomplish unless God intervenes. We need to leave a legacy. Focus on values. Don't just focus on rules and regulations, dos and don'ts. We must teach the kingdom values and principles.

Finally, do you have a clearly defined mission? *Who can you serve in your community? What are you trying to accomplish? What are the societal challenges that the church should be engaged with?* We need to answer these questions and meet these demands. We need to become more than just a religious entity that meets once a week. We are created, saved, called, commissioned, and commanded to serve God and His people in our communities. This is why God chose us: to serve God and His people. Just as the Israelites forgot their chosen status, we have forgotten our chosen status and have become an attractional church or an educational church. We cannot continue to be merely an attractional organization or institution.

When you study the early churches in the first century, the four walls did not define the church. The church was not a place, with a set time when they met on a weekly basis. But since then, we have become systematic and mechanical religious practitioners. We are inward focused instead of outward focused. We've become a "self-serving churchianity," instead of serving God and His people. We are not being "church" in our communities and in the world.

We must become a missional church, missional educational institutions, and missional hospitals—Seventh-day Adventists are a missional church movement. Wherever we are as individuals, or collectively as a church, we must live out the kingdom values and principles in order to create a long-term sustainable community that develops and engages.

After hearing one of my lectures, someone came up to me and said, "That sounds great in the city. But I live in the suburbs, and that's not relevant where I live." But I want to share what Stephen T. Um and Justin Buzzard said: "Not only do the suburbs receive culture shaped by the city, they receive *people* shaped by the city. And, though they have relocated to the suburbs, these individuals likely work in the city, are fed a cultural diet delivered to their doorstep by the city, succeed in the suburbs based on skills acquired in cities, and shape their lives and the world around them with the ideologies acquired during their formative years in the city."[15]

There is no separation between city and suburban life. We are all connected. Christianity is something people have to see, smell, touch, feel, and hear through our individual life and the unified church. If we don't demonstrate the love of God, but only proclaim the good news, it's not a complete picture.

Timothy Keller shares four essential attributes of being a missional church:[16]

First, a missional church is *evangelistic*. Keller says, Evangelistic means that "the work of God's Spirit in the world [is] to restore all creation" and reconcile broken relationships. This is why we embrace and engage in holistic ministries to reach the community—to demonstrate the love of God and to proclaim the good news. We must provide relief to individual and community developments, and reform our society.

Second, a missional church is *incarnational*. It is a model "where Christians live geographically close to each other, create a thick and rich community among themselves, and then become deeply involved in the civic and corporate life of their neighborhood or city." We must be involved and engaged with our communities and with other civic organizations to discover the needs of our society and begin to serve them in Christ's name—and only as a by-product will the church membership benefit. There will be a natural and organic church growth.

For example, while we are serving the homeless people in our communities, we interact with our affluent community. Through our demonstrated passion, commitment to serve, and desire to make a difference, nonbelievers in our affluent community begin to show their appreciation and desire to serve the homeless people with us. There are many sincere people in our communities simply looking for opportunities to serve. We should create these opportunities for people to serve. Sometimes, we think we are the only vegetarians in the world, but there are a lot more out there.

Third, a missional church is *contextual*. Keller says we should be involved with "deep reflection on culture and discovering creative ways of communication and church practice." Church must be relevant to the postmodern culture and post-Christendom reality. When mingling with the people outside the walls of the church, we also have to be sensitive of their complex environments. We have to know the people in our communities.

The Hedgehog Concept could be interpreted as an internal analysis to measure strengths, weaknesses, threats, and opportunities of an organization.[17] This concept was shared by Chinese General Sun Tzu in *The Art of War* during the fifth century B.C. His strategies can be summarized in two conceptual frameworks: know your people, and know your enemy. Let's say I'm a general and I'm taking you to war. I need to know your strengths and weaknesses. See opportunities and threats. Know how many weapons we have, what war tactics you're familiar with. This is called internal analysis—knowing our passion, competencies/skill sets, and resources (both tangible and intangible). We should have an inventory and church membership database.

Then know your enemy (I'm not saying your community is your enemy) and study your community. This is external analysis. You have to study your community and know who is out there. You have to know people and how to build the bridge between church and community.

Both Jim Collins and Sun Tzu emphasized the importance of leadership in organizational performance through business models and military tactics, and the importance of building capabilities of an organization through strategic internal and external analysis. We might contextualize both concepts into a program cycle in order to enhance its performance evaluation: (1) assessment/internal and external analysis, (2) goals, (3) program planning, (4) implementation, and (5) formative and summative evaluation.

The *assessment* is to identify high-priority goals that will serve as the basis for new or revised programs. Then an entity could decide the means to achieving previously selected goals. After initiating and implementing the program, conduct a formative or summative evaluation. A formative evaluation examines an ongoing program or project to decide if improvements are needed. A summative evaluation is conducted at the end of the program or project for funders, corporate sponsors, or other decision makers to determine the overall effectiveness of a fully developed program in order to decide whether to continue, expand, or drop the program.

It is to build organizational capacity systems, both internal systems and external relationships: internal systems to investigate mission, leadership, volunteers, technology, evaluation process, and infrastructure; and external relationships to investigate the status of current and potential funders, partners and sponsors, and constituents. It is about having a significant impact within the context of the values and beliefs cherished by people who support the organizational mission and purpose.

This is why organizational capacity building is a crucial component and is viewed in the context of an organization's objectives and values. It is about creating an organization that has the ability to make a serious impact on its desired mission.

By and large, the church is struggling with two sets of groups—the modernists and the postmodernists. The modernists are from the industrial and technological era. They focus on cooperation and see things in black and white; they have a small margin of error.

Postmodernists practice from the age of conceptualization, but they are willing to see beyond the black and white and see the gray. I'm not saying one is better than the other, but there are differences and we need to embrace the differences and learn to coexist. The church cannot be ruled or managed just by the modernists and completely ignore the postmodernists' viewpoints and worldviews, or vice versa.

I personally am a modernist; I'm concrete and sequential. I make decisions based on charts, numbers, and figures; you won't get a dime out of me with a sob story. I say, "I think, therefore I am." On the other hand, my wife is the total opposite of me, a postmodernist. She's abstract, right-brained, and random. She makes a decision based on feelings. She says, "I feel, therefore I know." The more you cry, the more you've convinced her. So the church requires both groups to work together. That's why God created the right and left brains.

But we have no patience for people who are different from us. Outside the church, the world doesn't function in the same "age." Some are living in the industrial/technology age mind-set, while others are in the conceptual age mind-set. It is important to know your community and correctly identify their mind-set in order to meet their needs in a relevant way.

Last, a missional church is *reciprocal and communal.* Keller says that a missional church calls us to a careful reworking of both our theology and our practice. First, in theology, sin cannot be seen just as an offense against the Holy God vertically; we must also look at it in horizontal terms—sin as the violation of God's shalom in the world through selfishness, violence, injustice, and pride. The ramifications of sin are both vertical and horizontal; it affects our God and His people. In addition, "the [missional] church listens and learns what God is doing [in the community] and then gets involved."[18] Each member of the church must be involved and interact with their community, with humble minds, to listen and learn about their community, get to know their neighbors, pinpoint societal challenges, and get to know what their spiritual and holistic needs are.

When I talk and listen to people in the community, I can speculate whether they are modernists or postmodernists by the words they use. And when we speak modernist words to postmodernists (or vice versa), we are not reaching them. We are not speaking their language. Let's examine the choice of words from the two ages as representing the mind-set of societal expectations, behaviors, and practices. It is interesting to note the differences that we encounter. For example, Jill Friedman Fixler and Sandie Eichberg embrace a new vocabulary to reflect more accurately the philosophy and practice of collaborative volunteer engagement:[19]

Industrial Age Led by Modernists	Conceptual Age Led by Postmodernists
Management	Engagement
Recruitment	Cultivation and networking
Placement	Negotiation and agreement
Supervision	Support
Performance review	Performance measurement
Recognition	Acknowledgment
Retention	Sustainability

Why is understanding this difference so important or relevant in our community outreach ministries? Here is a prime example: I went to a country where 95 percent of the population is Muslim. A group of Americans was having an evangelistic series, and their banner had the word *crusade* on it. *Crusade* in a Muslim country? To the local people, *crusade* means Christian evangelism done tragically . . . "gone bad." These American evangelists had no sensitivity to the people they were trying to reach.

This lack of understanding and knowledge accentuates how bad we are at building personal relationships with others. In fact, in most cases, our relationship with non-Christians is largely superficial. Most of us occupy significant relationships outside of work, with other Adventists and Adventist activities. We live in an Adventist bubble.

Every Adventist must be a faithful servant of God for this missional church movement. We must reach out to everyone, sharing, caring, and proclaiming the good news of God's redemption. People need to see us as a sign of the kingdom of God on earth.

We must confront all divisions of race, gender, age, and culture, striving to realize justice and peace, upholding the integrity of creation. We must journey together as a people of prayer.

In the midst of confusion and loss of identity, we must discern the signs of God's purpose being fulfilled and expect the second coming of our God, our Lord and Savior, Christ Jesus. We must serve God and His people, expecting the healing of human community in hope and wholeness of God's entire creation.

"There is need of coming close to the people by personal effort," wrote Ellen White. "If less time were given to sermonizing, and more time were spent in personal ministry, greater results would be seen. The poor are to be relieved, the sick cared for, the sorrowing and the bereaved comforted, the ignorant instructed, the inexperienced counseled. We are to weep with those that weep, and rejoice with those that rejoice. Accompanied by the power of persuasion, the power of prayer, the power of the love of God, this work will not, cannot, be without fruit."[20] I believe that most Christians have divorced the teachings of Jesus from the methods of Jesus, and yet they expect the results of Jesus.

> "There is need of coming close to the people by personal effort."
> —Ellen G. White

In general, modernists tend to follow the industrial approach: (1) present the logical truth through the public evangelistic engagement, (2) convert people to accept the presented beliefs, and (3) when the individuals demonstrate the certain expected behaviors, then the individuals will be accepted into the fellowship of the church.

Modernists	Postmodernists
Logical Truth	Friendship
Conversion	Influence
Fellowship	Commitment

However, a postmodern society tends to focus on the following: (1) friendship—relationship-building environments, (2) through the trust relationship that has been established, individuals will begin to influence others with the values and principles of the kingdom of God, and (3) with a continual journey in relationship building, people will be connected to God and will commit to become devoted disciples.[21]

This is why Michael Horton says, "*The ministry of the church as an institution or embassy instituted by Christ*—identified by preaching, baptizing, communing and teaching everything Christ delivered—*is where disciples are made.* Worldly vocations are where disciples are sent."[22] For this mission, God has created us, saved us, called us, commissioned us, and commanded us to influence the world as salt and light—to turn the world upside down. He offers meaning, fulfillment, and significance in our lives.

We must overcome institutional myopia and cultural differences and see the wider world as the setting for our calling, commission, and commandment as Seventh-day Adventists. The mission of the church is about faithfully establishing and building the kingdom of God on earth, through community outreach ministries, until the second coming of our Lord, Christ Jesus.

We must connect people to God through evangelism and worship. We must connect people to one another through community and discipleship. We must connect people to the community through mercy and justice. And we must connect people to the culture through the integration of faith and work. We must connect people with their Creator and Redeemer.

Someone said, "The church begins when the worship ends." We are Seventh-day Adventists, not Seventh-day *Event*ists; we must live our lives as an extension of God's missional heart.

---

1. Bosch, *Transforming Mission*, 400.

2. George Bernard Shaw, http://www.goodreads.com/quotes/456466-i-am-of-the -opinion-that-my-life-belongs-to.

3. White, *Acts of the Apostles*, 9.

4. Kreider, " 'They Alone Know the Right Way to Live': The Early Church and Evangelism," 170.

5. Keller, *Center Church*, 285 (italics in the original).

6. Keller, *Center Church*, 284, 285.

7. Mahatma Gandhi, http://www.goodreads.com/quotes/22155-i-like-your-christ-i -do-not-like-your-christians.

8. Norella M. Putney and Vern L. Bengtson, "Theories of Aging," in *Encyclopedia of the Life Course and Human Development*, ed. Deborah Carr et al. (Farmington Hills, MI: Gale Group, 2008), 413–423.

9. Stephen R. Covey, *The 8th Habit: From Effectiveness to Greatness* (New York: Free Press, 2004), 12.

10. A. M. Kent and A. E. Kirby, "The Design of the Store Environment and Its Implications for Retail Image," *The International Review of Retail, Distribution and Consumer Research* 19, no. 4 (2009): 457–468.

11. Daniel H. Pink, *A Whole New Mind: Why Right-Brainers Will Rule the Future* (New York: Riverhead Books, 2006).

12. Pink, *A Whole New Mind*, 1–3.

13. Matt Rogers, "Contextualizing Theories and Practices of Bricolage Research," *The Qualitative Report* 17, no. 48 (2012): 1–17.

14. Eric O. Jacobsen, *The Space Between: A Christian Engagement With the Built Environment* (Grand Rapids, MI: Baker Academic, 2012), 193.

15. Stephen T. Um and Justin Buzzard, *Why Cities Matter: To God, the Culture, and the Church* (Wheaton, IL: Crossway, 2013), 31 (italics in the original).

16. Timothy Keller, *Serving a Movement: Doing Balanced, Gospel-Centered Ministry in Your City* (Grand Rapids, MI: Zondervan, 2016), Kindle edition, chap. 1.

17. Jim Collins, *Good to Great: Why Some Companies Make the Leap . . . and Others Don't* (New York: HarperBusiness, 2001), 90–119.

18. Keller, *Serving a Movement*, chap. 1.

19. Jill Friedman Fixler and Sandie Eichberg with Gail Lorenz, *Boomer Volunteer Engagement: Collaborate Today, Thrive Tomorrow* (Bloomington, IN: AuthorHouse, 2008), 12.

20. White, *Ministry of Healing*, 143, 144.

21. Paul Heelas with the assistance of David Martin and Paul Morris, *Religion, Modernity, and Postmodernity* (Oxford, UK: Blackwell, 1998).

22. Horton, *The Gospel Commission*, 231, 232 (italics in the original).

CHAPTER 4

Learning Through Serving

There is a medical clinic being built in Ensenada, Mexico. What is unique about the project is that the clinic is being built solely by Americans. As a matter of fact, several different groups of American Christians have gone to Ensenada to build the clinic as a short-term mission project. Each mission group goes and does a bit of work; the electrical work is done by one group, the plumbing by others, the drywall by a different group, and so on. The construction has been ongoing for the past five years, and it will take two more years to complete the project because of a lack of money and availability of volunteer workers. The project is totally reliant on Americans who will go during their spring, summer, and winter breaks. Building a medical clinic is important, but why will it take seven years to build? What is the real challenge in this situation?[1]

According to researchers Robert Priest, Terry Dischinger, Steve Rasmussen, and C. M. Brown, the number of Short-Term Mission (STM) participants is well over a million a year. This is derived from a national survey showing that 2.1 percent of the U.S. population has gone on an STM trip during the past year (2005), and 3.6 percent claimed to have gone on one when they were teenagers. These numbers indicate that more than 1.5 million U.S. Christians annually go on STM trips, and spend more than $1 billion in the process.[2]

An Ensenada native who was working as a translator for many different STM groups says, "I am thankful for them, because they come from so far away to help my city. I know what it is like to sleep where they are, because I spent a night at the ranch. It's not easy, much less after working a full day. But also I feel that sometimes, they [STM participants] don't help much. Sometimes, their help makes the community become lazier. They say, 'Ah, why should I work if an American group is going to come? They'll help, build, and provide what we need.' They don't turn to God." What is the real challenge in this situation?[3]

The major challenge is the internationalization of our community outreach ministry mind-set. David Livermore said that "colonization was primarily built upon the internationalization paradigm."[4] When we engage in community outreach ministries, we often don't value our community as assets. Therefore, our community engagement is more colonization than relationship building with people in the community.

As we approach our community or STM projects, perhaps we should incorporate an asset-based, community-engaged research strategy whereby community and church members work as equal partners. The South Side Health and Vitality Studies (SSHVS)—the research and evaluation arm of the University of Chicago Urban Health Initiative—developed a model to "(1) identify community priorities, (2) track community assets, (3) leverage community assets, (4) conduct research, and (5) generate new knowledge that is then used to reset priorities."[5]

When we don't value our community as assets, we will continually develop a colonization model of community outreach programs, such as "reaching hopeless" or "reaching helpless" types. I am not saying there are no hopeless or helpless people in our communities, but that passive viewpoints often result in negative connotations. We often neglect the importance of whole community engagement and dismiss the assets of our communities.

Let's say that someone has reached the fifth level of Maslow's Hierarchy of Needs, which is "self-actualization." They've realized personal potential, self-fulfillment, seeking personal growth, and peak experiences. This person could have no religious belief, no commitment to follow Jesus; however, in his or her mind, this person is neither hopeless nor helpless. In fact, this person might be seeking for opportunities to serve, might want to contribute to society, might want to make a difference. Nevertheless, because of our passive approach and negative attitude, the person rejects any involvement with us. They don't see and hear the colonization message as relevant to them. We need to create opportunities for people to serve in affluent communities and share inspirational messages and see them as assets, to collaborate with them.

We should adopt the asset-based community engagement principles into our community outreach initiatives and mission work: (1)

involving diverse community members in key decision-making processes, (2) building mutual respect and trust between the church and
the community, (3) addressing issues that are most important to the
community, (4) maximizing participation of and leadership by people
living in the community, (5) jointly learning and discovering—together
and from each other—the value of research for improving and sustaining community development, and (6) creating learning opportunities
by involving students, teachers, church, and community members.[6]

We must involve community members as a vital component of community outreach initiatives. Robert Linthicum indicates the three types
of churches in his book *Empowering the Poor*.[7]

First, the church *in* the community, which refers to location; members are not from the community and have little or no involvement in
the community. It is based on the internationalization paradigm based
on colonization siege mentality. May-Ellen Colón, director of Adventist Community Services International at the General Conference of
Seventh-day Adventists, says, "This type of church is like a salt shaker
inside a loaf of banana bread." Jesus says, "You are the salt of the earth"
(Matthew 5:13). However, we've lost our saltiness. Russell Burrill said,
"For too long Adventists have isolated themselves in safe havens and
ghettos, as if the rest of the world did not exist. That time has ended.
We cannot, we dare not live in apostasy any longer. It's time to enter the
community as individuals and as a church."[8]

Second, the church *to* the community, which refers to some sense
of responsibility to do something for the community; however, decisions about what the community needs are made without consulting
community leaders and members to find out what the community
needs. Colón says, "If we don't meet people in our communities and
seek to meet their real needs, what we sprinkle on the banana bread-
community may be downright inappropriate or irrelevant—like sprin-
kling garlic salt on banana bread."

Last, the church *with* the community, which sees mission to the community as a partnership, collaborates with the community leaders and
members, brings the ministry of the church out into the community,
and nurtures personal relationships with individuals in the community.
This is the church that asks the community leaders and members *What
does this community need?* and incorporates the community engagement
principles into their community outreach initiatives. Colón says, "In
this loaf, the salt is with the other different ingredients in the bread. It's
mixed in with them, flavoring and enhancing the resulting bread. Salt

does more good when it is mixed with ingredients different than itself."

This is why Linthicum urges the church to be intentionally engaged with the whole community as partners, including the public, private, and nonprofit sectors. We must see and approach our community as assets, not just being a service recipient. We need to seek partnership in our communities.

John Fuder, in his book *A Heart for the Community: New Models for Urban and Suburban Ministry*, recommends the following ten tips to exegete a community:[9]

1. *Go as a learner.* This requires humility, persistence, and the courage to push past your fears. We need to approach as students and listen to what community members are saying to learn about the community—its political environment, socioeconomic status, civic history, concerns, lifestyles, values, and challenges. Psychographics gives much more insight than demographics, insight we can obtain only through listening and talking to community members in person.
2. *Seek out an "informant."* Find an individual who is a gatekeeper, an insider, "someone who promotes peace" (Luke 10:6). This is someone who will let you in to his or her lifestyle or subculture, an expert who can teach you about his or her journey as "lived experience" in the community.
3. *Build a relationship.* As much as you can, be a "participant observer" in that person's life, culture, and activities. A relationship, growing into a friendship, is key because a trust bond is formed, and trust is the collateral of cross-cultural ministry. In the process, God works to break your heart for that community (Matthew 9:13; Luke 13:34).
4. *Use an interview guide.* It is helpful to work from an outline, even though you may not always stay on script.
5. *Analyze your data.* Depending on the formality of your community analysis, you will likely end up with some form of field notes. A crucial step is to examine your data for holes, patterns, and hooks. *What missing pieces could your informant provide? What interests, activities, or values recur? Is there anything that can help you enter your informant's world more deeply?*
6. *Filter through a biblical worldview. What scriptures speak to the information you are discovering? What does the Bible say about the activities, lifestyles, and beliefs in your neighborhood? What would Jesus*

do, or have you do, in response to the needs? A biblical framework is the strongest platform on which to mobilize your church/ministry/school to action.

7. *Expand into the broader community.* Your informant can act as a "culture broker" to give you entry into the additional lifestyles and subcultures within the broader community. As you learn to read your audience (become streetwise) and develop credibility in the neighborhood, you can leverage those relational contacts into greater exposure and deeper familiarity with the needs in your area.

8. *Network available resources.* As your awareness of the community grows, you will invariably feel overwhelmed by all there is to do! But you do not have to reinvent the wheel. *Is anyone else working with that audience? If so, can you partner with them? With whom can you share and gather resources and information?*

9. *Determine what God is calling you to do. With the knowledge you've picked up about your community, what do you do now? Plant a church? Start a new ministry? Refocus your current programs?* Much of your response will depend on your personnel and resources. But you are now poised to do relevant, kingdom-building work in your community.

10. *Continually evaluate, study, explore.* Our hope in Christ is firm, but everything and everyone around us in our world are in constant motion. *Is your neighborhood changing (again)? Who is God bringing to your community now? Is your church or ministry responsive to those opportunities? Are you winsome, relevant, and engaging?* We must always ask these questions, in every generation, to "serve the purposes of God" (see Acts 13:36).

Through practicing the above assets-based community engagements, we can find ways of working together more effectively not only internally, but also externally with community partners. Multidirectional collaboration will find new or better solutions to challenges in our communities and be able to do more with fewer resources. We can discover and create ideas for new services and community outreach ministry opportunities. As a result, the members of the church will feel energized and committed to tangible outcomes and developing real changes in our communities.

To change the concepts of community service and volunteerism, we must incorporate service-learning data as a critical mechanism, which is both reciprocity and pedagogy.[10]

The service and learning goals are equally weighted and each enhances the other. Service-learning is about making disciples by experiencing the saving and transforming power of Christ in our own lives in order to share it effectively with others. Linda Sax, Alexander Astin, and Juan Avalos indicated, "Service-learning is a learning strategy in which students have leadership roles in thoughtfully organized service experiences that meet real needs in the community. The service is integrated into the students' academic studies with structured time to research, reflect, discuss, and connect their experiences to their learning and their worldview."[11]

In addition, John Saltmarsh and others said, "Service-learning is the knowledge and the skills needed for . . . preparing students with the knowledge and the skills needed for [domestic and global] citizenship."[12]

Below are the Five Stages of Service Learning, as presented by Cathryn Berger Kaye:

In this design, service learning is seen as an engaging dynamic building on the core curriculum.

Investigation: Includes both the *inventory* or *profile* of student interest, skills and talents, and the *social analysis* of the issue being addressed. For this analysis, students gather information about the issue through action research that includes use of varied approaches: media, interviews of experts, surveys of varied populations, and direct observation and personal experiences. The action research typically reveals the authentic need that students will address.

Preparation: The service learning process moves the curriculum forward as students *continue to acquire content knowledge* and raise and resolve questions regarding the authentic need. They identify community partners, *organize a plan* with clarification of roles, responsibilities and time lines, and develop *skills* needed to successfully carry out the plan.

Action: Students implement their plan through *direct service, indirect service, advocacy,* and/or *research*. Action is planned with partners based on mutual understandings and perspectives, and aims for reciprocal benefits for all involved.

Reflection: Reflection is ongoing and occurs as a considered summation of thoughts and feelings regarding essential questions and varied experiences to inform content knowledge, increase self-awareness, and assist in ongoing planning. When students have varying modalities for reflection, they grow to identify their preferred ways to reflect and value the reflective process. This leads to students becoming reflective by choice.

Demonstration: Student demonstration *captures the entire service learning experience*, beginning with investigation, and includes what has been learned, the process of learning, and the service or contribution accomplished. Sharing this with an audience educates and informs others. Students draw upon their skills and talents in the manner of demonstration, often integrating technology.[13]

The methodology of service-learning dictates that a clear link exists between the service experience and the academic objectives of the course. In a service-learning experience, students learn not only about social issues, but also how to apply the new knowledge to action that addresses real problems in their own communities. Service-learning students are assigned challenging community tasks, which take into account the community's assessment of its own needs, strengths, and resources to be leveraged.[14]

Based on the above belief and conviction,

Campus Compact was founded in 1985 by the presidents of Brown, Georgetown and Stanford Universities and the president of the Education Commission of the States. In the mid-1980s, the media portrayed college students as materialistic and self-absorbed, more interested in making money than in helping their neighbors. The founding presidents believed this public image was false; they noted many students on their campuses who were involved in community service and believed many others would follow suit with the proper encouragement and supportive structures.

Campus Compact was created to help colleges and universities create such support structures. These include offices and staff to coordinate community engagement efforts, training to help faculty members integrate community work into their teaching and research, scholarships and other student incentives, and the institutional will to make civic and community engagement a priority. Today more than 98% of Campus Compact member campuses have one or more community partnerships, and more than 90% include service or civic engagement in their mission statements. These campuses are putting their knowledge and resources to work to help build strong communities and educate the next generation of responsible citizens.[15]

Here is an example of a conceptual framework of service-learning presented by Tania Mitchell in four levels of engagements:[16] (1) service, (2) learning, (3) service-learning, and (4) critical service-learning.

First, *service* is like cleaning up a riverbank by picking up trash.

Second, *learning* is like sitting in a science classroom looking through a microscope at water samples the students collected from the riverbank that they cleaned.

Third, *service-learning* is like students taking samples from local water sources, analyzing the samples, documenting the results, and presenting the scientific information to a local pollution-control agency.

Fourth, *critical service-learning* is like science students creating public service announcements to raise awareness of the human impact on water quality in order to change community attitudes and behaviors.

For example, a student could initiate a field education by partnering with a local family-owned small grocery store, to implement the service-learning by helping the owners develop an innovative marketing strategy. The student could also renovate the store with fellow students from various majors, such as engineering, interior design, and social work, to improve the condition of the store, improve its efficiency of service, and discover other areas of service that the store could provide, including community services. This relationship between the educational institution and the family will continue, even after this student who initiated the relationship graduates, because other students will continue the engagement. It is a lifetime commitment between the institution and family. Perhaps, if we continue this type of engagement with community members around all Adventist institutions, we will soon begin to see the impact and positive results in students' learning experiences, institutional reputation and growth, and betterment of the community.

Mitchell shares that critical service-learning is a distinct subset of service-learning. It is a fourth dimension that includes activism, where the church becomes the voice for the voiceless. It is examining the issues of power, privilege, and oppression. It is questioning the hidden bias and assumptions of race, class, and gender. It is working to change the social and economic system for equity and justice. It is the church becoming a defender of people who cannot defend themselves.

For example, the Sabbath is central to what it means to love God and love our neighbor as ourselves: God rested, and God commands us to honor Him through rest. But God commands us to extend and provide rest to everyone around us—especially to those who are unable to find rest for themselves.[17]

This is a perception similar to what we discussed in chapter 2 using Sider, Olson, and Unruh's four social ministry types: relief, individual development, community development, and structural change. We could see the importance of holistic engagement from relief to reform, providing not only immediate services, but also continuous transformation. Whole-community development and transformation is also based on the whole-person framework. This is why following the four social actions is essential for the missional church movement.

Service	Relief
Learning	Individual Development
Service-Learning	Community Development
Critical Service-Learning	Structural Change

In fact, the Social Change Model of Leadership Development is identified as the most applied leadership theory in the context of collegiate leadership development programs.[18] The social change model approaches leadership as "a purposeful, collaborative, values-based process that results in positive social change."[19]

The Social Change Model of Leadership Development was introduced by Helen Astin et al. in 1996 and has seven distinctive elements, the "Seven C's":[20]

1. *Consciousness of self*, in which an individual is aware of his or her own beliefs, values, attitudes, and emotions that motivate the individual to action
2. *Congruence*, or thinking, feeling, and behaving with consistency, authenticity, and honesty toward others
3. *Commitment*, the psychic energy that motivates the individual to serve and that drives the collective effort
4. *Collaboration*, to work with others in a common effort

5. *Common purpose*, which involves performing that collaborative work with shared aims and values
6. *Controversy with civility*, which recognizes two fundamental realities of any creative group effort: that differences in viewpoint are inevitable, and such differences must be aired openly but with civility if the group is to accomplish its task effectively while honoring individual group members
7. *Citizenship*, or the process whereby the individual (a citizen-learner, in the case of service-learning) and the collaborative group become responsibly connected to the community through the service activity.

According to Astin, "[A leader is] one who is able to effect positive **change** for the betterment of others, the community, and society. All people, in other words, are potential leaders. Moreover, the **process** of leadership cannot be described simply in terms of the behavior of an individual; rather, leadership involves collaborative relationships that lead to collective action grounded in the shared values of people who work together to effect positive change."[21]

The Social Change Model of Leadership Development is identified as the most applied leadership theory in the context of collegiate leadership development programs.[22] The social change model approaches leadership as "a purposeful, collaborative, values-based process that results in positive social change,"[23] and emphasizes two core principles:[24]

"First," says John Dugan, "leadership is believed to be inherently tied to social responsibility and manifested in creating change for the common good," and "second, the model is predicated on increasing individuals' levels of self-knowledge and capacity to work collaboratively with others."[25]

This model is an essential component of personal development in both leader development and leadership development. The term *leader development* is directed toward individuals to expand their capacity to be effective in leadership roles and processes.[26] The term *leadership development* is "the expansion of the organization's capacity to enact the basic leadership tasks needed for collective work."[27]

When we develop the first three elements—consciousness of self, congruence, and commitment—we could enhance the leader development, which is to expand the individual capacity in developing the leader's characteristics. And the next set of three elements—collaboration, common purpose, and controversy with civility—enhance the leadership development, expanding the organizational capacity. Then the individual will become more influential not only within the church, but also globally as a citizen of our society.

This social change model is also connected to the four elements of critical consciousness development, presented by Susan Cipolle:[28]

1. *Self-awareness*, which is developing a deeper awareness of self. It means to have a clear understanding of your level of privilege, your values, your role in society, and your responsibility to others.

2. *Awareness of others*, which is developing a deeper awareness and broader perspective of others. It means that church members are collaborating with different groups, with different backgrounds in the community. Members are out of their comfort zones and see injustice and inequity. Instead of doing inward-focused events, they begin to explore the opportunities to serve outside the walls of the church. As church members interact with the community members, they begin to hear personal stories and community challenges. Perhaps, through their interaction, the church members begin to see the community members as people, precious souls belonging to God, instead of projects or statistics or fishing pools. We will become less judgmental and more compassionate toward others. We will break down the barriers, the wall between the church and the community. We will break down stereotypes and begin to acknowledge injustice and inequity.

3. *Awareness of social issues*, which is developing a deeper awareness and broader perspective of social issues. As the church members inform themselves on social, economic, and political issues, they will begin to question their beliefs and develop solution-focused constructive services and community engagements.

4. *Ethics of service*, which is seeing one's potential to make a change. This is discipleship, where disciples make other disciples through positive service experiences, which enhances their feelings of competency and efficacy as difference-makers. The church members who have developed a clear sense of their values are more likely to live in accordance with their beliefs as disciples. Disciples who regard critical consciousness service as a part of their identity are more likely to connect their personal commitment to service with a profession where they can make a social contribution.

Research shows that when students take leadership in planning and directing service-learning experiences, academic and civic engagement increases. In addition, when they are given opportunities to voice their opinions and make presentations, students' public speaking and leadership skills improve, as they begin to see their role as change-agents.[29]

For example, Cipolle suggests the following questions be discussed when we are volunteering at a homeless shelter to implement the critical consciousness of service-learning:[30]

1. Knowledge—*What were your first impressions of the shelter?*
2. Comprehension—*How was this shelter similar to or different from what you expected?*
3. Analysis—*What parts of the experience have been most challenging to you?*
4. Synthesis—*What have you personally learned about yourself from this service?*
5. Evaluation—*What ideas do you have to help the situation of homelessness?*

Why is all this necessary? Because the missional church movement is about deliberately becoming developmental organizations, developing and equipping disciples who will make disciples of others. Robert Kegan and Lisa Lahey say, "Research shows that the single biggest cause of work burnout is not work overload, but working too long without experiencing your own personal development."[31]

The church must become a development organization where we make disciples through discipleship and personal development. We must create the culture and environment where individuals could learn to improve self-efficacy as difference-makers. When the church members and community members collaboratively engage in meaningful critical consciousness service-learning, we could connect people socially and spiritually inside and outside of the organizations.

Kegan and Lahey share that Deliberately Developmental Organizations (DDOs) are where "trust in truth" creates a culture in which it is OK to make mistakes, but unacceptable not to identify, analyze, and learn. They must constantly get in sync. Get the right people to recognize that people are built very differently; lead as someone who is designing and operating a machine to achieve the goal.[32]

On a recent mission trip, someone asked, "I don't understand. If unemployment is so high on the Native American reservations, how come we are painting their houses?" I am convinced that we must connect service (relief) to reform, and charity to social justice. We must empower the church members to better understand the world and have a positive impact on their family, neighbors, communities, and society as difference-makers. We must educate our church members to face and challenge the inequity and injustice in our world. We must equip the church members to embrace the differences and become dedicated and committed disciples, who will live their lives as change-agents and make a difference.

The church exists for this reason. The purpose of the church is to reach our communities for the glory of God, so we can make disciples who will join with us in this missional movement. God does not merely send the church on a mission. God is already on a mission, and the church must join God.[33]

Unfortunately, most Christians have divorced the teachings of Jesus from the methods of Jesus, and yet they expect the results of Jesus. Life-on-life relationship building was the method of Jesus. He dealt with each person as a precious soul belonging to God, Jesus Himself, and loved them, cared for them, and showed them how to follow in His footsteps. We must live life as He lived.

"Looking at the man, Jesus felt genuine love for him" (Mark 10:21, NLT). Author Laurie Beth Jones said, "Focus is one of the key attributes of a leader, and nowhere is it more powerful when applied to and on behalf of another human being."[34] As the scripture implies, Jesus' ability to build connections with people led to relationships rooted in love and trust. His ability to do this was remarkable because individual diversity can be one of the biggest challenges that any leader may encounter. Each individual has his or her own way of learning, adopting, processing, and applying new ideas and information. Acquiring skills that help individuals adapt to new learning strategies is necessary for leaders. Leaders must intentionally focus on learning how others process, what their values are, what their strengths and weaknesses are, and what their challenges and opportunities are. Understanding these components will nurture trusting relationships between leaders and those they lead and will make them more effective teachers and mentors.

Aubrey Malphurs emphasizes the *implementation* of thinking and

> "The process does not end with thinking through and discovering or rediscovering the core fundamentals. We must follow the thinking with action."
> —Aubry Malphurs

learning into systematic practice: "The process does not end with thinking through and discovering or rediscovering the core fundamentals. We must follow the thinking with action."[35] A fair approach in every employment situation is regular ministry appraisal. A supervisor or mentor identifies problems and deficiencies, as well as strengths. When this is done, the person knows where the problems lie and what he or she must do to improve.

As I teach and mentor in various settings, it has become more evident and clear to me that analyzing and facilitating an individual's learning variability is the key to a successful experience and will produce positive outcomes. Utilizing the technique of group brainstorming does not minimize an individual's strengths; instead, it enhances an individual's capacity. Through group brainstorming, leaders share decision-making opportunities, which nurture group support of an action because one individual did not make the decision.

I would like to urge you to apply the following learning models: Bloom's Taxonomy and Kolb's Learning Theory.

Bloom's Taxonomy emphasizes five learning strategies, which help to develop the ability to change our thought processes. A summary of Benjamin Bloom's theory includes the following:[36]

1. Comprehension: Involves the understanding and ability to interpret and communicate the meaning of given variables
2. Application: Implies the use of knowledge to solve problems
3. Analysis: Requires a learner to examine material or relationships of information of constituent parts and to arrive at some solution or response
4. Synthesis: Requires the learner to combine elements and parts into a unified entity
5. Evaluation: The most complex of all questions. It involves making judgments, appraising, choosing, assessing, measuring, and critically inspecting some ideas or object and determining its relative value or worth.

In addition to Bloom's Taxonomy, we must study and incorporate Kolb's Learning Styles in the service-learning implementation. Having developed the model over many years, David Kolb published his Learning Styles Model in 1984. The model gave rise to related terms such as Kolb's Experiential Learning Theory (ELT) and Kolb's Learning Styles Inventory (LSI).[37]

Academics, teachers, managers, and trainers acknowledge Kolb's Learning Styles Model and Experiential Learning Theory as truly seminal works, fundamental concepts toward our understanding and explaining human learning behavior, and helping others to learn.[38]

Kolb's Learning Theory sets out four distinct learning styles, which are based on a four-stage learning cycle. In this respect, "Kolb's model is particularly elegant, since it offers both a way to understand individual people's different learning styles, and also an explanation of a cycle of experiential learning that applies to us all."[39]

Kolb includes this "cycle of learning" as a central principle in his ELT, typically expressed as a four-stage cycle of learning, in which "immediate or concrete experiences" provide a basis for "observations and reflections." These "observations and reflections" are assimilated and distilled into "abstract concepts" producing new implications for action that can be "actively tested," in turn creating new experiences.[40]

Kolb's model works on two levels in a four-stage cycle:

1. Concrete Experience—(CE)
2. Reflective Observation—(RO)
3. Abstract Conceptualization—(AC)
4. Active Experimentation—(AE)

and a four-type definition of learning styles (each representing the combination of two preferred styles, rather like a two-by-two matrix of the four-stage cycle styles, as illustrated below), for which Kolb used the terms:

1. Diverging (CE/RO)
2. Assimilating (AC/RO)
3. Converging (AC/AE)
4. Accommodating (CE/AE).

Through the transforming social action and moral and civic responsibility, we should incorporate the critical service-learning in our community outreach ministries. Relief to reform and charity to critical consciousness is civic engagement for liberation.

At the end of day, the church is about proclaiming the good news of the kingdom of God, living in the kingdom of grace while on earth. To teach, baptize, and nurture new believers to become disciples—who will equip and develop other disciples; to respond to human needs in loving service; to transform an unjust structure of society through critical service-learning; and to strive to safeguard the integrity of all creation and sustain the lives on earth by liberating them in Christ.

This is why Jesus died, so our sins are forgiven; He has risen, so death is defeated. He has given us direct access to the kingdom of heaven, the kingdom of glory, and He has commanded us to obey—"Go and make disciples of all nations."

Once we get new members in the church door, the challenge is keeping them. Every time a new member is lost from a local church, it's not just that member; it's also the goodwill of the member generated toward the Adventist Church among his or her friends and family.

Perhaps we could adopt the principles below, developed by Campaign Consultation, Inc.[41] If a church adheres to these principles, new members as community outreach volunteers are more likely to stay. I have replaced the word *volunteer* with *member* to illustrate my viewpoints.

- Principle: *Members* stay if their tasks and procedures are clear.
  - How do you equip and develop new members as disciples?
  - What materials do they receive to clarify their tasks and procedures?
  - What areas of confusion exist? How do you know?
- Principle: *Members* stay if they feel welcome and appreciated.
  - What do you do to ensure that church leaders and members welcome new members?
  - What do you do to recognize and reward them for their support?
- Principle: *Members* stay if they bond to someone within the organization.
  - What opportunities do members have to get to know staff and other volunteers? What opportunities do your assignments offer?
  - Do you use teams or buddy systems to accomplish goals?
  - How can you ensure that members feel connected to others?
  - Does your unit socialize outside of worship times?
- Principle: *Members* stay if they receive feedback that connects their job to program success.
  - How do church leaders monitor and help develop members' competencies?
  - Does your church employ mentoring?
- Principle: *Members* stay if they have a voice in the organization.
  - Are you open to suggestions and feedback from your members?
  - What opportunities do you create to receive feedback?

- ○ How do you involve members in planning new initiatives?
- ○ How do you know they are invested?
- Principle: *Members* are motivated by opportunities to learn new skills.
  - ○ What are the skills members can learn from their assignments?
  - ○ How can you identify the skills your members want to learn and continually allow them these opportunities?
- Principle: *Members* are motivated by opportunities to "change the world."
  - ○ How can you design community outreach ministries so that they see the opportunity to create change and make a difference?
  - ○ What ways can you identify and recognize members' ability and progress in creating change?

How can the principles mentioned above be employed practically, especially to assist new members through their first year? During an initial new membership orientation, we should find out what skills or interests the new member has. Here are some thoughts for new member retention:

- Fully embrace and complete the Adventist Learning Community's "Community Services & Urban Ministry Certification Program," available through https://www.adventistlearningcommunity .com/courses/107.
- Assign a mentor to the new member.
- Suggest a specialty ministry track related to the interest area.
- Assign a role (even if it is assistant to "assistant something"). The role does not have to be related to that particular ministry track. It does need to be something meaningful that the church needs and the new member can do or learn.
- Make sure the new member is invited to informal gatherings your church members normally go to, such as going for meals after the meetings; invite them to social gatherings outside of the regular church activities.
- Schedule a follow-up meeting within ninety days to see how the new member is progressing and integrating.

There are many successful ways to bring new members into the church ministry programs. Bringing that newbie on board may be the result of a one-time event. Keeping him or her, however, will require the recurring efforts of your entire congregation. A well-structured retention community outreach ministry plan through service-learning, executed with professional leadership, will guarantee strong retention results of your newbies.

Every member should be involved in service (relief), learning (individual development), service-learning (community development), or critical service-learning (structural change/social justice). Remember, relief to reform and charity to critical consciousness.

We must make an institutional commitment to critical service-learning in all aspects of our church engagements, including all of the Adventist local congregations, educational institutions, and health-care ministries.

When we can state that we have had positive experiences collaborating with our communities, and witness tangible impact and other evidences that support our efforts, we not only proclaimed the good news, but also demonstrated the love of God. And as a byproduct, we will have positive changes in our own institutions internally, especially a deeper and broader understanding of the purpose of our existence.

Let us develop personal development and learning environments!

---

1. *Missio Docs: Mexico* (Azusa Pacific University, 2007).

2. Robert J. Priest et al., "Researching the Short-Term Mission Movement," *Missiology: An International Review* 34, no. 4 (October 2006): 431–450.

3. *Missio Docs: Mexico*.

4. David Livermore, *Driven by Difference: How Great Companies Fuel Innovation Through Diversity* (New York: AMACOM, 2016), 134.

5. Community-Engaged Urban Health Research Methods and Applications, http://compact.org/resource-posts/community-engaged-urban-health-research-methods-and-applications/.

6. Adapted from the University of Chicago Urban Health Initiative (UHI), a model of community and university engagement.

7. Robert C. Linthicum, *Empowering the Poor* (MARC Publications, 1991), 21–30.

8. Russell Burrill, *How to Grow an Adventist Church* (Hart Books, 2009), 50.

9. John Fuder, " 'Exegeting' Your Community: Using Ethnography to Diagnose Needs," in *A Heart for the Community: New Models for Urban and Suburban Ministry*, ed. John Fuder and Noel Castellanos (Chicago: Moody Publishers, 2009), Kindle edition, chap. 3.

10. Andrew Furco, "Service-Learning: A Balanced Approach to Experiential Education," *Expanding Boundaries: Serving and Learning*, 1996, 2–6.

11. Linda J. Sax, Alexander W. Astin, and Juan Avalos, "Long-Term Effects of Volunteerism During the Undergraduate Years," *Review of Higher Education* 22, no. 2 (Winter 1999): 187–202.

12. Edward Zlotkowski, "Opportunity for All: Linking Service-Learning and Business

Education," in *Higher Education and Democracy: Essays on Service-Learning and Civic Engagement*, ed. John Saltmarsh and Edward Zlotkowski (Philadelphia: Temple University Press, 2011), 223, 224.

13. Cathryn Berger Kaye, "The Five Stages of Service Learning: A Dynamic Process," *Service Learning: A Teacher's Guide* (CBK Associates, 2014), http://www.cbkassociates.com/wp-content/uploads/2013/05/The-Five-Stages-of-Service-Learning.pdf; italics in the original.

14. Jan Torres and Ruth Sinton, eds., *Establishing and Sustaining an Office of Community Service* (Providence, RI: Campus Compact, 2000).

15. Campus Compact: Washington, "History," http://www.wacampuscompact.org/history.

16. Tania D. Mitchell, "Critical Service-Learning as Social Justice Education: A Case Study of the Citizen Scholars Program," *Equity & Excellence in Education* 40, no. 2 (2007): 101–112.

17. Bethany Hanke Hoang and Kristen Deede Johnson, *The Justice Calling: Where Passion Meets Perseverance* (Grand Rapids, MI: Brazos Press, 2016), 41.

18. Julie E. Owen, "Towards an Empirical Typology of Collegiate Leadership Development Programs: Examining Effects on Student Self-Efficacy and Leadership for Social Change" (PhD diss., University of Maryland, 2008), http://drum.lib.umd.edu/handle/1903/8491.

19. Quoted in Kristan Cilente Skendall, "An Overview of the Social Change Model of Leadership Development," in *Leadership for a Better World: Understanding the Social Change Model of Leadership Development*, 2nd edition, ed. Susan R. Komives, Wendy Wagner, and Associates (San Francisco: Jossey-Bass, 2017).

20. Helen S. Astin et al., *A Social Change Model of Leadership Development: Guidebook*, ver. 3 (Higher Education Research Institute, University of California, Los Angeles, 1996), 22, 23, http://www.heri.ucla.edu/PDFs/pubs/ASocialChangeModelofLeadership Development.pdf.

21. Astin, *Social Change Model of Leadership Development*, 16; boldface in the original.

22. John P. Dugan et al., "The Role of Social Perspective-Taking in Developing Students' Leadership Capacities," *Journal of Student Affairs Research and Practice* 51, no. 1 (2014): 1–15.

23. Quoted in Skendall, "An Overview of the Social Change Model of Leadership Development."

24. John P. Dugan et al., "Influences of Leadership Program Participation on Students' Capacities for Socially Responsible Leadership," *Journal of Student Affairs Research and Practice* 48, no. 1 (2011): 65–84.

25. John P. Dugan, "Group Involvement Experiences in College: Identifying a Thematic Taxonomy" (PhD diss., University of Maryland, 2008), 29, http://drum.lib.umd.edu/handle/1903/8045.

26. Ellen Van Velsor and Cynthia D. McCauley, "Our View of Leadership Development," in *The Center for Creative Leadership Handbook of Leadership Development*, 2nd edition, ed. Cynthia D. McCauley and Ellen Van Velsor (San Francisco: Jossey-Bass, 2004), 2.

27. Ibid., 18; Aoife McDermott, Rachel Kidney, and Patrick Flood, "Understanding Leader Development: Learning From Leaders," *Leadership & Organization Development Journal* 32, no. 4 (2011): 358–378.

28. Susan Benigni Cipolle, *Service-Learning and Social Justice: Engaging Students in Social Change* (Lanham, MD: Rowman & Littlefield, 2010).

29. Shelley H. Billig, "Unpacking What Works in Service-Learning," in *Growing to Greatness 2007: The State of Service-Learning*, ed. James C. Kielsmeier, Marybeth Neal, and Nathan Schultz (Saint Paul, MN: National Youth Leadership Council, 2007).

30. Cipolle, *Service-Learning and Social Justice*.

31. Robert Kegan and Lisa Laskow Lahey, *An Everyone Culture: Becoming a Deliberately Developmental Organization* (Boston: Harvard Business Review Press, 2016), Kindle edition, introduction.

32. Ibid., chap. 1.

33. Alan J. Roxburgh, *Missional: Joining God in the Neighborhood*, Allelon Missional Series (Grand Rapids, MI: Baker Books, 2011).

34. Laurie Beth Jones, *Jesus, CEO: Using Ancient Wisdom for Visionary Leadership* (New York: Hachette Books, 2001).

35. Aubrey Malphurs, *Advanced Strategic Planning: A New Model for Church and Ministry Leaders*, 2nd ed. (Grand Rapids, MI: Baker Books, 2005), 28.

36. Mary Forehand, "Bloom's Taxonomy," in *Emerging Perspectives on Learning, Teaching, and Technology*, ed. Michael Orey (2010), 41, 47.

37. Alice Y. Kolb and David A. Kolb, "Learning Styles and Learning Spaces: Enhancing Experiential Learning in Higher Education," *Academy of Management Learning & Education* 4, no. 2 (June 2005): 193–212.

38. Meena Chavan, "Higher Education Students' Attitudes Towards Experiential Learning in International Business," *Journal of Teaching in International Business* 22, no. 2 (2011): 126–143.

39. Abdul Razaq Ahmad, Norhasni Zainal Abiddin, and Wan Hasmah Wan Mamat, "Participant's Assessment Towards Human Development Adult Education Program in Malaysia," *Journal of International Social Research* 2, no. 6 (Winter 2009): 27.

40. J. Dankelman et al., "Fundamental Aspects of Learning Minimally Invasive Surgical Skills," *Minimally Invasive Therapy & Allied Technologies* 14, no. 4-5 (2005): 247–256.

41. David Chavis, "Strategic Factors for Building Community: The Five C's Community, Connections, Control, Cash, & Collective Action," (Baltimore: Campaign Consultation, 2006).

PART III

HOW—How Do We Change Our Way of Thinking and Working?

CHAPTER 5

How to Measure the
Effectiveness of Ministry

Have you wondered if your ministry is effective? Whether your ministry will be viable in the future? How do you know if your participation is imperative? We can't keep doing the same old, same old and expect to see any changes in our communities, not to mention in our personal spiritual growth.

David G. Winter claims that successful leaders and managers must use power—to influence others, to monitor results, and to sanction performance. The Performance Evaluation and Assessment (PEA) is an inevitable component of leadership. Therefore, leaders should utilize the opportunity strategically to build trust between superiors and subordinates, and organizations and customers. The process ensures accountability and responsibility, with a commitment to serve in better ways and to trust in each other's strength.[1]

The PEA also accommodates the culture of change. Through its process, directly and indirectly, participants are motivated to change. Understanding the strengths and weaknesses and the ability to incorporate enhancement to improve oneself will benefit organizationally. It brings high participatory involvement of people and their organization. In addition, through its process, you can identify tangible outcomes that people could measure successfully.

However, even though we understand the importance and value of its evaluation and assessment, often it is a difficult task to implement properly. This is because often its performance measurement tools become a popularity contest or opportunity to bring negative criticism in public, based on one's behavioral attitude. It is extremely important to structure the PEA strategically in order to truly measure the process and outcomes. *Are the organization's mission, goals, and objectives consistent with its program and financial allocations? Is the organization incorporating multicultural and intergenerational involvement? How is the organizational sustainability?* Much careful thought and strategy are required up front, maximizing the benefits of evaluation and assessment.

The bottom line is that we cannot avoid evaluations. Whether we are in education, business, ministry, or nonprofit management, we must evaluate the viability of a program.

We are living in an emerging world, and change is inevitable.[2] There are demands that churches and parachurch organizations should demonstrate tangible impact, not just do events and activities. Church is not exempt from the pressure to discover which ministry or service really makes a difference in the community outreach ministries or an individual's life. Members want performance measures so they can hold church leadership accountable, as it is done for private- and public-sector leadership.

For-profit organizations define their success based on the bottom line because their primary goal is to generate revenue.[3] However, the mission for nonprofits, such as a church, is to bring about changes in societal values, in order to make the world a better place to live, with values of the kingdom of God and biblical principles.[4] Its measure of success is not how much profit it makes but the extent to which it makes a difference.

Nonprofit organizations are seeking not only outputs in measurable results but also the outcome and impact as to how they made a difference in an individual's life, and the impact of how the community was transformed because of their influence in society. Performance measurement is to create new social values in making the world a better place to live. Individuals in the community are looking for ways to give back to society and to be engaged in community support. Moreover, they are looking to do it in a way that is convenient but at the same time publicly demonstrate their support in providing opportunities to serve God and His humanity.

Harry P. Hatry offers a list of measurements for public-sector performance. He suggests that by incorporating these performance measurements, the public-sector leadership will accomplish greater results and enhance their credibility:

1. Respond to elected officials' and the public's demands for accountability.
2. Make budget requests.
3. Do internal budgeting.
4. Trigger in-depth examinations of performance problems and possible corrections.
5. Motivate.
6. Contract.
7. Evaluate.
8. Support strategic planning.
9. Communicate better with the public to build public trust.
10. Improve.[5]

Hatry is convinced that to improve the condition of society is the fundamental reason for performance measurement, and indicates it is intended to make program improvements that lead to improved outcomes.

Robert D. Behn also presents eight purposes that public managers have for measuring performance:

1. Evaluate.
2. Control.
3. Budget.
4. Motivate.

5. Promote.
6. Celebrate.
7. Learn.
8. Improve.

This is different from Hatry's list, which focuses on an individual's purpose to improve performance.[6]

The Purpose	The Public Manager's Question That the Performance Measure Can Help Answer
Evaluate	How well is my public agency performing?
Control	How can I ensure that my subordinates are doing the right thing?
Budget	On what programs, people, or projects should my agency spend the public's money?
Motivate	How can I motivate line staff, middle managers, nonprofit and for-profit collaborators, stakeholders, and citizens to do the things necessary to improve performance?

Promote	How can I convince political superiors, legislators, stakeholders, journalists, and citizens that my agency is doing a good job?
Celebrate	What accomplishments are worthy of the important organizational ritual of celebrating success?
Learn	What is working or not working?
Improve	What exactly should someone do differently to improve performance?

As the public sector focusing on impact and improvement of quality of life and environments, a church cannot measure the success by numbers only, such as the number of memberships or how many people attend the church. How many local churches do we have, or educational institutions, or health-care networks?

We must incorporate performance measurement in our public evangelism and community outreach ministries. Performance measurement is a systematic way to evaluate our effectiveness and efficiency of proclaiming the good news, and a way to create new social values in making the world a better place to live. Therefore, the focus is on the results of local impact and implementation, not the charity.

The missional church movement is not only proclaiming the good news through public evangelism but also demonstrating the love of God through community outreach ministries. In our ministries, we cannot prioritize which is more important than the other. It is not enough to count what we have done (for example, how many goods we distributed, people we served). We need to focus on making a difference in the lives of individuals and whole communities by increasing their knowledge, enhancing their skills, and influencing their attitudes and behavior. We must demonstrate our faithfulness to God's cause by fulfilling the duty to reach those around us.

As a missional church movement, we must learn how to apply performance measurement to our ministries to accomplish systemic changes, which will result in more effective and efficient ways to improve others' lives. Andrea Anderson describes how and why a set of activities should be part of a highly focused program or a comprehensive initiative, and leaders should lead early, expecting intermediate and long-term outcomes over a specified period. Furthermore, nonprofits should ask *why they exist. For whom do they exist? Who has a stake in the problem?* In addition, *What has to be changed?*[7]

The Theory of Change Approach to Evaluation (TCAE) gained popularity and wide acceptance in the 1990s through its innovative use in the evaluation of Comprehensive Community Initiatives (CCIs).[8] The basic description of a TCAE was defined by Carol Weiss. Essentially, Weiss proposed that TCAE requires that the designers of an initiative articulate the premises, assumptions, and hypotheses that might explain the how, when, and why of the processes of change.[9]

A logic model is a flowchart that depicts the inputs, activities, outputs, outcomes, and impact associated with a program.[10] Logic models (similar to TCAE) have been used in program planning and evaluation since the 1980s, preceding the popularization of TCAE.

Anderson describes logic models as placing greater emphasis on the representation of actual program components: the basic inputs, outputs, and outcomes of programs.[11] According to Anderson, TCAE is a description of how and why a set of activities should be part of a highly focused program or a comprehensive initiative, and expects to lead early, intermediate, and long-term outcomes over a specified period.

As a practical methodology for performance measurement, I would like to introduce the W. K. Kellogg Foundation's Logic Model as a road map guideline and measurement tool. The W. K. Kellogg Foundation's *Logic Model Development Guide*, an invaluable resource for planners and evaluators, provides a different perspective on the relationship between logic models and TCAE.[12]

In this guide the authors describe three types of logic models: Theory Approach Models (TAMs), Outcomes Approach Models (OAMs), and Activities Approach Models (AAMs). According to the classification, TAMs emphasize the theory of change that has influenced the design and plan for the program and are used to illustrate how and why the program will work. OAMs describe the program's anticipated outcomes or impacts over time, going from short-term to intermediate to long-term outcomes. AAMs describe program implementation, providing the specific phases and steps for program operations. From this perspective, theories of change are one type of logic model.

The W. K. Kellogg Foundation's Logic Model provides constituents with a road map describing the sequence of related events connecting the need for the planned program with the program's desired results. Mapping a proposed program helps you visualize and understand how human and financial investments can contribute to achieving your intended program goals and can lead to program improvements.[13] You can download the complete document and study it. I find it to be a really practical tool: http://wkkf.org/resource-directory /resource/2006/02/wk-kellogg-foundation-logic-model-development-guide.

Adaptation of this model results in a useful tool for both planning and evaluating community services. Use of the logic model can help missional church movement leaders to implement changes that are necessary to deliver high-quality and relevant community outreach ministries. This model is useful for planning as well as measuring the success of a program after it has happened.

The W. K. Kellogg Foundation's Logic Model uses strategic thinking and process to measure three variables:

1. **Efficiency:** the degree to which a program or service has been beneficial in relationship to its resources.
2. **Effectiveness:** the degree to which goals have been reached.
3. **Impact:** the degree to which a program or service resulted in changes in our community and individually. It is to measure both quantitative and qualitative success of our ministries.

The logic model has five major components; the first three are quantitative measurement, and the other two are qualitative measurement. Let me walk you through the five basic logic model components, which illustrate the connection between your planned work and your intended results:

1. ***Inputs*** include the human, financial, organizational, and community resources a program has available in order to make it work.
2. ***Program activities*** are what the organization does with the resources. Activities are the processes, tools, technology, and actions that are an intentional part of the program implementation. These may include *products* (producing promotional materials and educational curricula), *services* (education and program activities, counseling or health screening), and *infrastructure* (networks, relationships, partnerships, and capacity used to bring about the desired results).
3. ***Outputs*** are the direct results of program activities and may include types, levels, and targets of services delivered by the program. Outputs portray the volume of a program's actions, such as products created or delivered, number of people served, classes held, and so on.

Inputs, *program activities*, and *outputs* are quantitative data. Quantitative measurements focus on numbers. Quantitative data measures the *efficiency* of the program.

4. **Outcomes** are the specific changes in a program participant's knowledge, skills, attitudes, behavior, and level of functioning expected as a result of the program activities. Outcomes measure the result of the services on individuals. Ask: *What happened to individuals who participated in the program? Have we improved their knowledge, enhanced their skills, and influenced their attitude and behavior?* Effective change requires long-term commitment. Short-term outcomes should be attainable within one to three years, while longer-term outcomes should be achievable within a four- to six-year time frame. The logical progression from short-term to long-term outcomes should be reflected in *impact*, occurring within about seven to ten years.

As an example, let me illustrate individual-, organizational-, and community-level learning outcomes:

Expected Individual-, Organizational-,
and Community-Level Learning Outcomes

INDIVIDUAL OUTCOMES	SHORT-TERM IMPACTS	LONG-TERM IMPACTS
Leadership growth:	Organizational-level change:	Community-level change:
Increased knowledge	Increase in professional capacities (accountability, commitment, trust)	Increased influence and recognition of church in relevant social areas
Enhanced in skills	Providing vital services	Increased partnerships between community members and the church
Shift in attitude	Clear mission-driven goals and objectives	Increased cross-organization and sector participation in the church Community needs and expectations met by programs and services offered through holistic church-community partnerships

5. ***Impact*** is the fundamental intended change occurring in organizations, communities, or systems as a result of program activities within seven to ten years (such as improved conditions and
increased capacity). Impact often occurs after the conclusion of
project funding. For example, in short-term: *What will happen to
your organization?* In long-term: *What will happen to your communities?*

Outcomes and *impact* are qualitative data. Qualitative measurements
focus on people's experiences, behaviors, attitudes, and so forth. Qualitative data measures the *effectiveness* of the program.

The logic model will help to enhance organizational capacity to effect *change* in people's lives. By focusing on outcomes and impacts, you
will clarify the organization's mission and vision, and measure their
effectiveness.

Effectiveness (Qualitative) = Outcomes + Impacts

In addition, by focusing on inputs, activities, and outputs, an organization can better clarify its goals, objectives, and long-term strategies
to implement its programs. This helps the organization to measure its
efficiency.

Efficiency (Quantitative) = Inputs + Activities + Outputs

When an organization can measure its effectiveness and efficiency, it
can demonstrate its capacity in a tangible manner.

Capacity = Effectiveness + Efficiency

To effectively apply its theory of change, there must be changes in
the way of thinking and the way of working. In general, churches/non-
profits have concentrated on quantitative success, focusing on input,
activities, and outputs. We often ask and report how many people we
serve, how many goods have been provided, and what services we have
delivered. However, what society expects and demands are the results of
the impacts from their activities and events.[14]

Churches/nonprofits are not exempt from these demands and should
demonstrate the real impact of how community contributes and makes
a difference in individuals' lives. Therefore, churches should alter the
process, rather than focusing on quantities of programs. The entity
must seek the big picture first: the impact—how society influences the
church and the transformational engagements experienced collectively.

When *implementing* the logic model to plan a community outreach ministry, I encourage you to use the components of the logic
model in the following sequence (this is not the same sequence of the

W. K. Kellogg Foundation's Logic Model, but you will see the beneficial rationale for its modification): (1) impact, (2) outcomes, (3) activities, (4) outputs, and (5) inputs.

For example, let's say we are planning a stop-smoking seminar for our community, so we incorporate the W. K. Kellogg Foundation's Logic Model in this community outreach ministry:

Step 1: *Impact*—Stephen Covey says to begin with the end in mind.[15] That is why we start our plan focusing on the desired impact: *What is our vision of the impact on the community from this stop-smoking seminar? Will it decrease health-care costs? Will it eventually reallocate tax money for other areas of human services, such as education, housing, and employment? Will we have healthier people and neighborhoods? Can you think of other benefits to the community because of fewer smokers?* These are all examples of the *impact* part of the logic model. *How will this community be different five years from now, ten years from now, because of our faithful presence in these communities, through our long-term sustainable community outreach ministries?* The impact is like a dream, which becomes a challenge, inspiring and motivating us to be engaged, involved, and to contribute selflessly. Throughout the Bible we see God's intervention. God wants us to have a vision, which captures the commitment among people. Proverbs 29:18 says, "Where there is no vision, the people perish" (KJV).

In addition, today's knowledgeable workers need to know that what they do is significant. Peter F. Drucker advocates that companies that help their employees with this sense of significance create a far more productive work environment.[16] Try to ask people in the community to identify what the church stands for. I can guarantee you that most communities are clueless about what the church stands for or sometimes don't even know we are there.

People need to know the big picture (the end in mind)—knowing why we do what we do; we must pray and dream for the societal changes that we will create in our communities. *What are we trying to accomplish?* Any dream that we have, we won't be able to accomplish unless God intervenes.

Step 2: *Outcomes*—How to influence an individual life holistically— their physical, social, mental, and spiritual well-being. Conduct a preassessment and postassessment of the participants in the stop-smoking seminar; assess their knowledge, skill sets (degree of willpower to refrain from smoking by exercise, diet, etc.), and attitudes regarding smoking. Compare the results from before and after the seminar. *What changes happened in the individuals' lives as a result of the seminar? Have we increased their knowledge, enhanced their competencies/skill sets, and influenced their attitudes?* In addition, we should follow up with each participant in three months, six months, nine months, and twelve months—to assess any changes in their knowledge, skill sets, and attitudes.

Why do we do this? We are doing two things. First, we are collecting research-based and evidence-based data, which will demonstrate the program's results (especially important when we are seeking collaborative partnerships within the community in any of the three sectors: government, private/business/for-profit, and nonprofit/human services). We must demonstrate the program's value—its dependability, trustworthiness, accountability, effectiveness, and so on. We cannot approach our communities without having researched evidence-based data that validates the program's integrity and success. We have to earn the right and privilege to seek collaborative partnerships in our communities.

Second, we are building a personal relationship with the participants and their family members. As we engage with them through the continual assessments, we get to know them and their family members in a personal way. We learn their joys, concerns, and challenges, and perhaps we can be with them through a difficult journey in life (funeral, sickness, unemployment, divorce, youth at risk, etc.). We can also celebrate their birthdays, graduations, successes, accomplishments, and more. Through this ongoing personal relationship development, we are building a trust relationship between the church and the community. Through this trusted relationship, we will earn the right and privilege to share the good news with them.

On a side note, in my humble opinion, the messenger is just as important as the message itself. When the messenger is known, and the messenger's values and integrity are unbreakable, the messenger becomes dependable and trustworthy—and the message will also become real.

The outcome results are more than statistical data and qualitative study; they are about building relationships with people in our communities through these sustainable long-term community outreach ministries.

Step 3: *Activities*—Designing programs and services based on a needs analysis of the community. *What are the relevant ministries to meet* *the needs of the community?* Activities are not the same as the traditional "events" and should include the following three key elements:

1. *Products:* Develop or acquire advertising materials and educational tools such as videos, brochures, and PowerPoint presentations to present facts about smoking in a seminar format. Products are the educational tools and information that we will utilize in stop-smoking seminars.
2. *Services:* Develop a plan for promotion and advertisement. Meet every night for five days (the "when") at the local church, elementary/middle/high school, public facilities, or businesses (the "where") and conduct the stop-smoking seminars, implement a buddy system, and employ a self-checklist (the "how"). Services generate the action plan on stop-smoking ministry—who, what, when, where, with what? It is an action plan.
3. *Infrastructure:* Form collaborative partnerships in the community with hospitals, schools, public health care, and other faith groups to gain support and involvement in this stop-smoking program. Support from these community partnerships builds sustainable credibility for your stop-smoking ministry and demonstrates the effectiveness and efficiency of your ministry.

Step 4: *Outputs*—How the programs and services have been delivered and supported. How many people participated and how many partnerships were established internally and externally?

In planning mode (projected results): *Whom do we aim to reach with the advertisement and the stop-smoking seminar? How many people do we project will participate? How many handouts will we need? How many times will the seminars be conducted? How many community partnerships do we aim to establish?*

In measuring actual results: *How many people actually participated? How many seminars were actually conducted? How many handouts were distributed? How many community partnerships were established, and how did they participate in the stop-smoking program?* It's a breakdown of the results from the activities—the number of products, services, and infrastructure.

Step 5: *Inputs*—What are the resources that each entity has in tangible format, including competencies and skill sets that are required to fulfill the goals and objectives. *What are the resources we need for the stop-smoking program, such as finances, presenters, facilities, equipment, and advertising materials? What do we need to do this ministry?*

This is the last question that we ask ourselves, not the first. We often ask ourselves, as the first and foremost important question, Do we have enough money, people, equipment, and so on? In fact, as we implement the logic model, we learn that this should be the last question. When we are faithful to the process—the journey through the logic model—God will connect us with the resources. God will provide through His faithful servants, not only in the church but also in our communities.

I hope that you will be able to apply the logic model to planning and measuring the organizational performance of your community outreach ministries. When you are faithful to the process, you will be successful at the end and you will be able to enhance your organization's ability to fulfill its mission. Maya Angelou said, "I did then what I knew how to do. Now that I know better, I do better."[17]

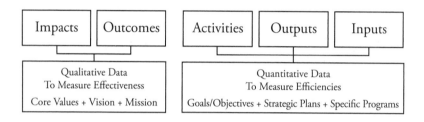

A friend had a water project in Kenya. The first three years he had graphics and tables with figures of the villages they were in, how much water they were pumping, and so forth. It was all about numbers. But by the fourth and fifth years, donations were declining. He hired a consultant team to figure out why donations were down. The consultant told him, "You focus on efficiency numbers (quantitative data, quantitative success), but offer no stories, no quality of ministry."

And my friend replied, "This is a water project; there are no stories. Results are just numbers."

But the consultant said, "You need to tell stories, not just numbers." So he focused on two things: crime rate and educational opportunities.

Some of you are probably wondering, *How is a water project connected to crime and education?* In any given village, the ones bringing water to their homes are the young girls. As the young girls travel back and forth from these water supplies, the probability of these girls being attacked and raped is high. So these water pumps allow water to be brought directly to their homes, and the girls can focus on going to school. So indirectly, the crime rate goes down, and educational opportunities go up. Donors were excited and interested in these results, and they were willing to aid in these efforts.

In addition, he also created a virtual learning community. Let's say I am a mathematician or an accountant, and I don't have the opportunity to go to a foreign country to serve as a long-term missionary. But I can choose to teach math over the internet through Skype or GoToMeeting (there are several mechanisms). I can schedule and teach over the internet at my convenience.

And not only do I teach over the internet; I also have an opportunity provided by the organization (once a year) to go to the foreign country and interact with my students. The students I had only seen online, I can now play with, eat with, teach, and learn from. How do you think I felt about the ministry? I loved my trip and came home contagiously passionate about my service. I came back and told my colleagues about these opportunities and the impact we can make on these students on the other side of the world. We can be a part of the solution in the global challenges of education, hunger, poverty, and more.

We can also apply the same principle to our communities. When we can't figure out the necessity of our community, we're just doing events. Internal systems and external relationships need to administer organization capacity methodically. Internal systems investigate mission, leadership, volunteers, technology, evaluation processes, and infrastructure. External relationships investigate the status of current and potential funders, partners and sponsors, and constituents.

There are demands that faith-based nonprofit organizations should report on the results they achieved, not just the activities and finances. We should discover which services really make a difference, to focus on activities, scale up activities and services, and achieve a greater impact. There are more demands to form strategic alliances with other nonprofit organizations and with the public and private sectors to achieve objectives. Furthermore, there is an expectation that nonprofit organizations will become more sustainable, rather than lurching from one challenge to the next.[18]

Throughout the project, we should ask:

1. What are the leading-edge approaches to enhance our ministries?
2. What should leaders and members be doing differently to enhance the performance of our ministries?
3. How can the impact of the church be significantly increased?

This is why evaluation is a critical element of organizational growth and enhancement.

Donald Kirkpatrick presents a system for evaluating the effectiveness of the training program. The system assesses four types of information:[19]

1. The reactions of the participants
2. The learning they achieved
3. Changes in their behavior
4. The final business results

Evaluation may not be an exciting process, but it is the only way to assess the effectiveness of a program. By demonstrating that the training program has been productive and beneficial to the participants, credibility of the training program will be validated and able to sustain its reason for existence. The chart below "shows the definitions of these types of data presented at levels that represent an update, modification, and addition to the four levels developed by Kirkpatrick."[20]

Evaluation Levels and Measurement Focus[21]

Evaluation Level	Measurement Focus
1. Reaction and planned action	Measures participant satisfaction with the leadership development and captures planned actions
2. Learning	Measures changes in knowledge, skills, and attitudes
3. Application and implementation	Measures changes in on-the-job behavior and progress with application
4. Business impact	Captures changes in business impact measures
5. Return on investment	Compares program monetary benefits to the program costs

Reaction and Planned Action. At Level 1, the participant reacts to the leadership development program. A variety of data items are collected at this level, with particular focus on measures such as the

- relevance of the leadership development program to the current work assignment;
- importance of the leadership development program to job success;

- intent to use what is learned in the leadership development program;
- amount of new insights gained from the leadership development process; and
- effectiveness of the facilitator.

Although other measures can be developed, these are the critical ones that often correlate with the application of leadership development.

Learning. At Level 2, learning is measured usually on self-assessment scales. As new knowledge, skills, insights, and understandings are developed, it is important to measure the changes. Without learning, there will be no behavior change. Learning can be measured with skill practices, simulations, case studies, assessments, and traditional objective tests.

Application and Implementation. At Level 3, the application of leadership development is monitored. Here, the actions, steps, processes, and behaviors are captured during and following the leadership development program. The most common method is to use 360-degree feedback from other managers and direct reports. At this level, participants report on progress with action plans, individual projects, team projects, specific applications, and initiatives.

Business Impact. At Level 4, business impact measures are the consequences of the new behavior and program application. The leadership development program should influence one or more key measures, such as productivity, quality, costs, time, customer satisfaction or job satisfaction.[22]

The first three levels of Kirkpatrick's evaluation—reaction, learning, and performance—"are largely soft measurements; however, decision-makers who approve such learning processes prefer results (returns or impacts). Jack Phillips (1996), who probably knows Kirkpatrick's four levels better than anyone else does, writes that the value of information becomes greater as we go from motivation to results. That does not mean the first three levels are useless, indeed, their benefits are being able to locate problems within the learning package:"[23]

- The motivation evaluation informs you [of] how relevant the learning process is to the learners (it measures how well the learning analysis processes worked). You may have all the other levels correct, but if the learners do not see a purpose for learning and performing, then they probably won't perform it.
- The learning evaluation informs you to the degree of relevance that the learning process worked to transfer the new skills to the learners (it measures how well the design and development processes worked).
- The performance evaluation informs you of the degree that [the learners'] skills actually transferred to their job (it measures how well the performance analysis process worked).
- The results evaluation informs you of the *return* the organization receives from supporting the learning process. Decision-makers normally prefer this *harder* result, although not necessarily in dollars and cents. For example, a study of financial and information technology executives found that they consider both hard and soft returns when it comes to customer-centric technologies, but give more weight to non-financial metrics (soft), such as customer satisfaction and loyalty.[24]

"This results measurement of a learning process might be met with a more balanced approach or a balanced scorecard . . . , which looks at the impact or return from four perspectives:"[25]

- Financial: A measurement, such as an ROI [return on investment], that shows a monetary return, or the impact itself, such as how the output is affected. Financial can be either soft or hard results.
- Customer: Improving an area in which the organization differentiates itself from competitors to attract, retain, and deepen relationships with its targeted customers.
- Internal: Achieve excellence by improving such processes as supply-chain management, production process, or support process.
- Innovation and Learning: Ensuring the learning package supports a climate for organizational change, innovation, and the growth of individuals.[26]

In 2007, Daniel Stufflebeam and Anthony Shinkfield pointed out the distinction between formative and summative evaluations as follows:

Formative Evaluations for Improvement. Formative evaluations provide feedback for improvement. They are prospective and proactive. They are conducted during the development of a program or its ongoing operation. Formative evaluations offer guidance to those who are responsible for ensuring and improving the program's quality and, in doing so, should pay close attention to the nature and needs of the consumers. Stufflebeam points out that formative evaluations assess and assist with the formulation of goals and priorities, provide direction for planning by assessing alternative courses of action and draft plans, and guide program management by assessing implementation of plans and interim results.[27]

Formative evaluation is to enable people and agencies to make judgments about the work undertaken; to identify their knowledge, attitudes, and skills, and to understand the changes that have occurred in these; and to increase their ability to assess their learning and performance.[28]

Summative Evaluations for Accountability. Summative evaluations typically occur following development of a product, completion of a program, and the end of a service cycle. These are retrospective assessments of completed projects, established programs, or finished products.[29]

Summative evaluations are useful in determining accountability for successes and failures, informing consumers about the quality and safety of products and services, and helping interested parties increase their understanding of the assessed phenomena.[30]

Robert Stake made an interesting observation regarding the relationship between formative and summative evaluations: Formative evaluations are closely connected to "insiders" (i.e., program developers), while summative evaluations are of more interest to "outsiders" (i.e., the potential users of the developing [or developed] programs).[31]

Summative evaluation is to enable people and agencies to demonstrate that they have fulfilled the objectives of the program or project, or to demonstrate that they have achieved the standard required.[32]

Eleanor Chelimsky makes a similar distinction between the two primary types of evaluation, which she calls Evaluation for Development (i.e., the provision of evaluative help to strengthen institutions and to improve organizational performance) and Evaluation for Accountability (i.e., the measurement for results or efficiency to provide information to decision makers).[33] Chelimsky adds to the discussion a third general purpose for doing evaluations: Evaluation for Knowledge (i.e., the acquisition of a more profound understanding about the factors underlying public problems and about the "fit" between these factors and the programs designed to address them).[34]

In addition, communities are pressuring churches to form strategic alliances with other nonprofit organizations and the public and private sectors to achieve objectives that are ever more demanding.

In order to achieve a greater impact on society, it is imperative to work with all three sectors: public, private, and nonprofit. Collectively and corporately, all three sectors should share resources and form a collaborative alliance to bring about real and intended results. As we engage the whole community, we have the potential for a greater impact.

I was blessed and privileged to receive an award, "Forty Under 40, Dayton's Brightest Young Business Leaders," because I had a wonderful opportunity to incorporate the above conviction. Truly, it was God's inspiration that led to its conceptual framework and implanting strategy. Dayton, Ohio, is a unique city in many ways and located in a strategic area of the state.

Individuals who are struggling with substance abuse or are mentally challenged, but desiring to transform their lives, will journey to Cincinnati, Ohio. Why Cincinnati?

The city developed a well-organized, systematic approach to support the homeless people in becoming self-sufficient and self-supporting within a year or two:

1. The individuals will go through the specific rehabilitation programs, based on their needs.
2. Individuals will be educated and equipped with traits and skill sets to be employable.
3. These individuals will be connected to possible employers and able to access financial-aid programs to secure low-income housing.
4. Through individual savings and financial management programs, they soon become self-reliant.

Each individual works with a social worker throughout the life-changing process.

So, as you can see, many people would like to go to Cincinnati and change their lives, and the majority travel from Chicago, Columbus, or Indiana. As they travel from their home to Cincinnati, they travel through Dayton, Ohio, which is about fifty miles north of Cincinnati.

When individuals arrived in Dayton, they would contact the local churches in the community for help (such as food, clothing, gas, and a place to stay). This happened frequently, and individual churches responded to those in need. But as we observed the situation, we noticed that some individuals were not so truthful with their needs and were going church to church, taking advantage of any compassionate ministries.

At that time, there were six Adventist churches that were part of the Ohio Conference, and two churches that were part of the Allegheny West Conference, as well as the Kettering Medical Center, Kettering College of Medical Arts, and Spring Valley Academy. These entities came together to deal with the situation collectively, along with the Good Neighbor House, a local Adventist Community Services center.

First, each Adventist congregation and entity contributed financial support to assist the homeless people in Dayton. Second, we took the money and went to local businesspeople (private sector—grocery stores, gas stations, motels, etc.) and asked for their support of our effort. We would pay one dollar for their two dollars' worth of contribution—but more often than not, the merchants said we were doing a good work and gave us five dollars' worth of service, and we provided them with a simple donation letter. Third, the free service vouchers that we received from the merchants we disseminated throughout the local police and fire stations (public sector), and asked them to distribute the vouchers according to the needs.

When the homeless person contacts the local church, the church informs them to visit the nearest police or fire station. What happens? Only individuals who are honest about their needs will show up at the police or fire station for the free vouchers. We eliminated duplicated services through collaborative efforts. Soon, other faith-based groups joined the effort, more merchants became involved, and it became a citywide, whole-community engagement. We simply connected the dots between public, private, and nonprofit sector/church.

There needs to be a significant impact within the context of the values and beliefs cherished by people who support the organizational mission and purpose. This is why Organizational Capacity Building (OCB) is a crucial component and viewed in the context of an organization's objectives and values.[35] It is about creating an organization that has the ability to make a serious impact on its desired mission.

OCB can be measured. To demonstrate the effectiveness and efficiency of the organization, you use the following equations:

Capacity = Effectiveness + Efficiency

Effectiveness (Qualitative) = Outcomes + Impacts

Efficiency (Quantitative) = Inputs + Activities + Outputs

When an organization is able to demonstrate its capacity, financial support from internal constituents and the community will happen as a by-product. We often think that financial resources are the first priority—that without finances, nothing can be accomplished. It is not. We must demonstrate our values and capacity first; then the support will follow. By demonstrating our values and capacity, we will earn a reputation for dependability and the trust of our communities.

This is why the values of each organization are crucial components of success, and value-driven marketing is a global phenomenon. It has developed new ways for business and nonprofit to collaborate and achieve mutual benefits. It includes product sales, promotions, and program-driven collaborations between companies and nonprofits, which include churches. It is also known as "cause marketing"[36]—a mutually beneficial collaboration that aligns the power of a company's brand, marketing, and people to a charitable cause's brand and assets, to create shareholder and societal values, connect with constituents, and publicly communicate values. It could be also interpreted as "social marketing"[37]—public service marketing that takes the cause beyond awareness to impact the way people act and think, while building brand equity and preference and publicly being a part of a company's commitment to social responsibility.

The focus is on the cause, not the charity, in local impact and implementation. It is important to identify the intersection of interests in church, corporation, and public stakeholders. It is the intersection where societal needs and corporate goals meet and can come together for mutual benefits. The relationship is based on mutual respect, open communication, and trust. You must be transparent, authentic, and honest.

To develop financial sustainability, we must keep in mind the three fundamental principles of fund-raising: faith, relationship, and service.

Faith—It is God who works in people's hearts, motivating them to give. *It is my responsibility to pray for them and ask God to work in their hearts.*

Relationship—This is about developing a lifelong relationship between the constituency and the organization, building personal relationships and having heart-to-heart communication.

Service—Develop and create opportunities for people to serve God and His people. It is to provide giving opportunities, to assist people in wise estate planning, and to provide counsel on total giving.

Through value-driven marketing strategies, we could reach the public in nontraditional places: shopping centers, car dealerships with ads, marketing places, products, events, and so on. Mission-driven marketing offers visibility, public awareness of issues, and an innovative way to reach a broad base of consumers with important educational and action-oriented messages. That is why selling pink jelly beans for the American Cancer Society works. Instead of being passive—"come and see"—we must be proactive, reaching out to people where they are.[38]

Value-driven marketing should focus on building a relationship and making a connection with constituents that involves their active participation and engagement. Peter C. Brinckerhoff presents the essential components of this relationship,[39] such as:

Employees—helps attract, retain, and create employee pride.

Community—puts a human face on company/organization, giving a license to operate.

Shareholders—a corporation is a for-profit company and has a responsibility to return on investment to shareholders.

Value-driven marketing can enhance a company's ability to achieve profit. Trades and suppliers will require nonprofits to look for new sources of revenue and resources to achieve their mission goals. Customer appeal is directed to socially conscious consumers, time-crunched consumers, women, and teens as an efficient way to reward companies for their community values and to communicate their own values.

Value-driven marketing products are sales driven and transactional based. The products can be directly tied to a nonprofit's brand through a percentage of sales going for a cause, allowing consumers to do good while buying goods. For example, KaBOOM!, a nonprofit organization dedicated to building a great place to play within walking distance of every child in America, collaborated with Ben & Jerry's to create KaBerry KaBOOM! ice cream (a blueberry and strawberry flavor combo). The American Red Cross and Home Depot created and distributed ready gear and emergency kits. One of the most common ways is to add a donation onto purchases—add a dollar or more to support the local hospital campaign to send underprivileged children to summer camp, or contribute to the food banks.

Cause program involvement and support is used as a signature piece to build the company's name, brand, and reputation while helping the nonprofit organization to advance their mission. It is not about raising funds; it is about creating new values and transforming our society.

This is why we must develop reasons why someone would support our organization. If your organization does not have a solid case, your philanthropy's potential is limited. As in science, an organization must work on the following components to enhance its capacity:[40]

- Mission: *Why do we exist? What is the need and why is it important to meet that need?* Your mission statement defines the human or societal needs that are central to your organization and explains why those needs must be addressed.
- Goals: *What are we going to accomplish? How is our mission carried out?*
- Objectives: *How are we going to accomplish goals?*
- Programs/services: This area lists your entire program and what is involved in providing the program or services. It is based on community assessments, which are based on interviews, data research, surveys, and so on.
- Staff: *Who is going to accomplish the programs and services? What are our staffing needs?* As part of your planning process, you should identify the job descriptions of all your staff members. *Do we have the human resources to accomplish our mission and goals?*
- Governance: *What is the structure of our organization?* Governance is leadership, and it is a core issue for philanthropic success and campaign planning. *Do we have an active board? Will they lead our next campaign successfully?*
- Facilities: *Where are we providing the services? Do we have the physical resources to address our mission?* If you don't, you must strategize how you plan in the future to address those needs.
- Finances: A thorough knowledge of the financial state of your church is essential in determining your readiness for fundraising. You need to let your constituents know that you are responsible with the funds you currently have. Keep excellent financial statements, annual reports, gift-income progress reports, and cost-analysis reports.
- Strategic planning: You need a current and regularly updated statement of needs. *What are our program needs? Are they endowment or capital needs? What is a strategic game plan for the next three to five years?* You must have a game plan for your organization.
- Evaluation: It is to uphold the accountability within your internal and external constituents. If you are ready to encourage philanthropy, you must also know how your organization and its philanthropic program will be accountable to those who support it.
- Communication: *Is the public aware of our programs and services,*

and do they support them? You should explore multiple opportunities to utilize the media, promotions, and campaigns.
- History: History substantiates who you are and why you exist. You should develop an organizational portfolio demonstrating your capacity and competencies.

The Joint Committee on Standards for Educational Evaluation (1981, 1988, 1994, 2003) defines evaluation as "the systematic assessment of the worth or merit of an object." By *worth*, it refers to a program's combination of excellence and service in an area of clear need within a specified context.[41] *Merit* assesses quality—that is, an object's level of excellence—and asks, *Did the object do a good job of what it was intended to do?*

Evaluation can be viewed as a structured process that creates and synthesizes information intended to reduce the level of uncertainty for stakeholders about a given program or policy.[42] Evaluation is the provision of information about specified issues upon which judgments are based and from which decisions for action are made.[43] It is about either *proving* something is working or needed, or *improving* a practice or a project.[44] James C. McDavid says the intent of evaluation is to answer questions or test hypotheses, the results of which are then incorporated into the information data used by those who have a stake in the program or policy. The first often arises out of accountability to funders, managers, and, crucially, the people they are working with. The second is born of a wish to do better.[45] We look to evaluation as an aid to strengthen our practice, organization, and program.[46] It is the collection and analysis of quality information for decision makers.[47] Evaluation may be of individuals, programs, projects, policies, products, equipment, services, concepts and theories, or organizations.

Again, why measure performance? It is to transform this world to have the values and principles of the kingdom of God. It is to create an impact in our society and make a difference in people's lives. It is not a simple evaluation. It is a process—a faithful journey—to fulfill the responsibility as disciples of our Lord, Jesus Christ.

The Great Commission in Matthew 28:18–20 addresses God's mission in the world as two components: (1) to reconcile the broken relationship between God and His children, through baptism of the triune God, and (2) to transform the world into the kingdom of God, through life-changing experiences as His disciples.

If the church is missional in nature, community outreach is not optional. Community outreach becomes the primary reason for the church's existence. We must earn the respect and privilege to share the truth of our Savior and Lord, Jesus Christ. To earn respect, we must be real. We need to share with people new hope, motivating them, treating them with dignity, and giving them respect in Jesus Christ. Christians must be about building the kingdom of God. We must be serious about our mission and its impact.

Both program evaluation and performance measurement are increasingly seen as ways of contributing information that informs performance management decisions. Performance management, which is sometimes called results-based management, has emerged as an organizational management approach that depends on performance measurement.[48]

We should ask ourselves, *What are the leading-edge approaches to enhance our ministries? What should leaders and members be doing differently to enhance the performance of our ministries? How can the impact of the church be significantly increased?*

We must develop a strategic process to seek effective and efficient community outreach ministries.

Let's make *real* changes!

---

1. David G. Winter, "A Motivational Model of Leadership: Predicting Long-Term Management Success From TAT Measures of Power Motivation and Responsibility," *The Leadership Quarterly* 2, no. 2 (1991): 67–80.

2. Thomas J. Tierney, "The Leadership Deficit," *Stanford Social Innovation Review* 4, no. 2 (Summer 2006): 26–35.

3. Kent D. Fairfield and Kennard T. Wing, "Collaboration in Foundation Grantor-Grantee Relationships," *Nonprofit Management and Leadership* 19, no. 1 (Autumn 2008): 27–44.

4. David Livermore, *Leading With Cultural Intelligence: The New Secret to Success* (New York: AMACOM, 2009).

5. Harry P. Hatry, *How Effective Are Your Community Services? Procedures for Performance Measurement* (2007).

6. Robert D. Behn, *Rethinking Democratic Accountability* (Washington, DC: Brookings Institution Press, 2001).

7. Andrea A. Anderson, *The Community Builder's Approach to Theory of Change: A Practical Guide to Theory Development* (New York: Aspen Institute Roundtable on Community Change, 2005).

8. James P. Connell et al., eds., *New Approaches to Evaluating Community Initiatives: Concepts, Methods, and Contexts* (New York: The Aspen Institute, 1995).

9. Carol H. Weiss, "Nothing as Practical as a Good Theory: Exploring Theory-based Evaluation for Comprehensive Community Initiatives for Children and Families," in ibid., 65–92.

10. Leonard Bickman, "The Functions of Program Theory," *New Directions for Program Evaluation,* no. 33 (Spring 1987): 5–18.

11. Anderson, *Community Builder's Approach to Theory of Change.*

12. W. K. Kellogg Foundation, *Logic Model Development Guide* (Battle Creek, MI: W. K. Kellogg Foundation, 2004).

13. Anderson, *Community Builder's Approach to Theory of Change.*

14. Tierney, "The Leadership Deficit."

15. Stephen R. Covey, *The 7 Habits of Highly Effective People* (New York: Simon & Schuster, 1989).

16. Peter F. Drucker, *Management Challenges for the 21st Century* (Oxford, UK: Butterworth-Heinemann, 2007).

17. Maya Angelou, http://www.goodreads.com/quotes/9821-i-did-then-what-i-knew -how-to-do-now.

18. Stephanie Gajewski et al., "Complexity and Instability: The Response of Non-governmental Organizations to the Recovery of Hurricane Katrina Survivors in a Host Community," *Nonprofit and Voluntary Sector Quarterly* 40, no. 2 (2011): 389–403.

19. Donald L. Kirkpatrick and James D. Kirkpatrick, *Evaluating Training Programs: The Four Levels*, 3rd ed. (San Francisco: Berrett-Koehler, 2006).

20. Jack J. Phillips and Patti Phillips, "Measuring Return on Investment in Leadership Development," in *The Handbook of Leadership Development Evaluation*, ed. Kelly M. Hannum, Jennifer W. Martineau, and Claire Reinelt (San Francisco: Jossey-Bass, 2007), 142.

21. Ibid., 143.

22. Ibid., 142, 143.

23. Don Clark, "Kirkpatrick's Four Level Evaluation Model," updated October 5, 2015, http://www.nwlink/~donclark/hrd/isd/kirkpatrick.html.

24. M. Hayes, "Just Who's Talking ROI?" *Information Week*, February 2003, 18.

25. Clark, "Kirkpatrick's Four Level Evaluation Model."

26. Robert S. Kaplan and David P. Norton, *The Strategy-Focused Organization: How Balanced Scorecard Companies Thrive in the New Business Environment* (Boston: Harvard Business School Press, 2001).

27. Daniel L. Stufflebeam and Chris L. S. Coryn, *Evaluation Theory, Models, and Applications*, 2nd ed. (San Francisco: Jossey-Bass, 2014).

28. Benjamin S. Bloom, J. Thomas Hastings, and George F. Madaus, *Handbook on Formative and Summative Evaluation of Student Learning* (McGraw-Hill, 1971).

29. Daniel L. Stufflebeam, "CIPP Evaluation Model Checklist," March 17, 2007, https://www.wmich.edu/sites/default/files/attachments/u350/2014/cippchecklist _mar07.pdf.

30. Stufflebeam and Coryn, *Evaluation Theory, Models, and Applications.*

31. Robert E. Stake, "Program Evaluation, Particularly Responsive Evaluation," *Evaluation Models*, Evaluation in Education and Human Services, vol. 6 (Dordrecht: Springer, 1983), 287–310.

32. Bloom, Hastings, and Madaus, *Handbook on Formative and Summative Evaluation of Student Learning.*

33. Eleanor Chelimsky and William R. Shadish, eds., *Evaluation for the 21st Century: A Handbook* (Thousand Oaks, CA: SAGE Publications, 1997).

34. Ibid.

35. Jim Collins, *Good to Great and the Social Sectors* (Random House, 2006).

36. Paul N. Bloom et al., "How Social-Cause Marketing Affects Consumer Perceptions," *MIT Sloan Management Review* 47, no. 2 (2006): 49.

37. Peter C. Brinckerhoff, *Mission-Based Marketing: Positioning Your Not-for-Profit in*

an Increasingly Competitive World (Hoboken, NJ: John Wiley & Sons, 2010).

38. Christian Grönroos, "Value-Driven Relational Marketing: From Products to Resources and Competencies," *Journal of Marketing Management* 13, no. 5 (1997): 407–419.

39. Peter C. Brinckerhoff, *Mission-Based Marketing: An Organizational Development Workbook* (Hoboken, NJ: John Wiley & Sons, 2003).

40. I learned these from the North American Division Philanthropic Service for Institutions. For more information and tremendous fund-raising resources, please visit http://www.philanthropicservice.com/.

41. Daniel L. Stufflebeam and Anthony J. Shinkfield, *Evaluation Theory, Models, and Applications* (San Francisco: Jossey-Bass, 2007), 9, 325–365.

42. James C. McDavid and Laura R. L. Hawthorn, *Program Evaluation & Performance Measurement: An Introduction to Practice* (Thousand Oaks, CA: SAGE Publications, 2006).

43. Elizabeth Wolfe Morrison, "Newcomer Information Seeking: Exploring Types, Modes, Sources, and Outcomes," *Academy of Management Journal* 36, no. 3 (June 1, 1993): 557–589.

44. Patricia J. Rogers and Bob Williams, "Evaluation for Practice Improvement and Organizational Learning," in *The SAGE Handbook of Evaluation*, ed. Ian F. Shaw, Jennifer C. Greene, and Melvin M. Mark (London: SAGE Publications, 2006), 76–97.

45. McDavid and Hawthorn, *Program Evaluation & Performance Measurement.*

46. Chelimsky and Shadish, *Evaluation for the 21st Century.*

47. Stufflebeam and Coryn, *Evaluation Theory, Models, and Applications.*

48. McDavid and Hawthorn, *Program Evaluation & Performance Measurement.*

CHAPTER 6

Leadership and Discipleship Development

What is leadership? Since the beginning of humankind—perhaps, even in heaven—*leadership* has been an integral part of all lives, even among the animal kingdom. To some degree, it has been somewhat of a myth, searching for true leadership, trying to define its identity throughout each century and history. In general, today's society defines the attributes of leadership as being a hero, a remarkable accomplisher, a motivator, an influencer, and so on, and we've even gone so far as to develop various leadership programs, workshops, publications, and books to equip a person or groups to become more effective. However, Joseph Rost shares the interesting observation that the word *leadership*, used in scholarly and popular publications, organizational newsletters and reports, as well as the media, means very different things that have little to do with the considered notion of what leadership actually is.[1] How is leadership defined? Are you focusing more on performance rather than character? Or is it both? Could leadership be defined as servant, instead of ruling class?

The leadership curriculum builds on the best insights from a variety of fields, including the discipline of leadership itself. Over the past thirty years, leadership education has evolved as a field of study with theoretical frames, conceptual models, standards of practice, and diverse pedagogical strategies.[2]

Rost, author of *Leadership for the Twenty-First Century*, made pathways to define leadership in academia. He sorted through the classic models of leadership, which he referred to as *managerial* or *industrial* models, and brought awareness to the relational, ethical, and process models of leadership, which he referred to as *postindustrial*.[3]

Largely focused on managerial leadership and political leadership until the 1980s, many leadership educators, motivated by James Burns's book *Leadership* (1978), embraced a transforming, ethical approach to leadership development.[4] The role of the follower was elevated, and the focus shifted to all people involved in the leadership process.[5]

Also in the early 1980s, the new growing body of organizational behavior literature informed leadership education programs.[6] Key models on how students learn, including David Kolb's Experiential Learning Model[7] and Marcia B. Baxter Magolda's Learning Partnership Model, set the foundation for structuring leadership programs characterized by learning and development outcomes.[8]

The body of academia on leadership theory continues to expand. In 2011 Peter Northouse published a student workbook, *Introduction to Leadership: Concepts and Practice*, to accompany his text written in 1997, and in 2008 James Kouzes and Barry Posner framed their work for students with *The Student Leadership Challenge: Five Practices for Exemplary Leaders*.

Kouzes and Posner's research that led to their 1987 book *The Leadership Challenge* and five exemplary practices provided a framework that captured the attention of leadership educators. Kouzes and Posner present five practices of a servant leader:[9]

1. *Model the way*—The ability to establish principles concerning how goals will be attained and the ways individuals interact, characterized by role-modeling good behavior, as well as setting expectations.
2. *Inspire a shared vision*—The capacity to envision, passionately communicate, and enlist support for future possibilities for organizations and groups.
3. *Challenge the process*—A willingness to examine and change the status quo, characterized by informed risk-taking and willingness to learn from mistakes.
4. *Enable others to act*—The ability to engage others in shared processes characterized by mutual investment, collaboration, and empowerment.
5. *Encourage the heart*—The capacity to recognize and celebrate accomplishments—both individual and group.

Additional research has linked the five exemplary leadership practices to perceptions of effective leadership, as well as demonstrated that students can increase the frequency of these skills through a variety of educational interventions.[10] This can serve as a powerful personal learning tool regarding one's leadership behaviors and how others perceive them.[11]

However, Peter Northouse does offer cautions about solely relying on the five practices. The model is designed as a starting point for leadership development and can be used to establish an important common language and help people expand their capacity to be engaged in leadership. When used in isolation, however, the model is largely perceived as leader-centric and lacking a complex consideration of context and capacities necessary for group- versus individual-level interactions.[12]

As the field of leadership education continues to evolve, both new and seasoned leadership professionals "must rely on skills associated with lifelong learning as they continuously encounter demands that require the integration and application of new knowledge."[13]

One aspect complicating the understanding of the definition of leadership is the nature of the term itself. "The terms *leader* and *leadership* are often bandied about with little to no substantive explication."[14] Dennis Roberts described leadership as "a leader who knows self well; can analyze and diagnose environments; is able to be flexible and appropriately adapt to the situation; and who, in the end, has the foresight and imagination to see what the organization can be."[15]

The term *leader development* is directed toward individuals to expand their capacity to be effective in leadership roles and processes,[16] and the term *leadership development* is "the expansion of the organization's capacity to enact the basic leadership tasks needed for collective work."[17]

Leader development is directed toward cultivating the character traits of integrity, determination, transparency, passion, humility, and so forth in an individual. Leadership development is expanding a leader's organizational and managerial ability to establish direction, motivate and inspire people, plan, solve problems, budget, organize, and so on. We must invest in both leader development and leadership development.

Leadership theories relating to Adventist organizations
For a Christian, servanthood is an essential requirement in possessing spiritual traits and gifts. God gave various spiritual gifts to the church, such as discipling, prophesying, teaching, and ministering (Ephesians 4:11–13). Regardless of each individual's calling, servanthood is the basis for all gifts that encourages others to serve, to give, to help, to be merciful, and to be hospitable. These traits are more critical especially for the church than for the corporate world. As our Lord Jesus Christ served, we

ought to serve one another. Ledbetter, Banks, and Greenhalgh discuss the phrase "servant leadership": " 'Leadership' remains the key term and 'servant' the qualifier. What we need today are not, as is so often suggested, more *servant leaders* but, properly understood, more *leading servants*."[18] Ellen White writes, "Kneeling in faith at [the foot of] the cross, he [the sinner] has reached the highest place to which man can attain."[19]

Therefore, discipleship development should attempt to equip participants to become *leading servants* who understand how to motivate and lead, to identify and exploit opportunities, to create values and understand ethics, and to understand principles and issues in Christian leadership.

Jesus lived His life as a humble servant: "Just as the Son of Man did not come to be served, but to serve, and to give his life as a ransom for many" (Matthew 20:28). The bottom line of the Christian journey is to be servants of God. Our ambition is not leadership but servanthood. We must become leading servants as Christian disciples, who order their lives around mission and who believe they are responsible for fulfilling the Great Commission.

As we grow in Christian discipleship, we as servant leaders will focus more on the *servant* aspect of servant leadership. As we serve beyond the walls of our church, we will ask ourselves these questions:

- *How is our dependability? Are we doing what we say we will do?*
- *How is our timeliness? Are we doing things when we say we will do them?*
- *How is our empathy? Are we doing things with an eye to the needs of the community?*
- *How is our tangible evidence? Are we doing things in ways that let communities know service has been performed?*

Leadership theories specifically relating to Adventist organizations include (1) industrial theory, (2) postindustrial leadership theories, and (3) relational leadership theory. This chapter will describe each theory as it relates to church ministries in organizational behaviors.

Within the categories of leader and leadership development, many different types of leadership are being developed. One of the first distinctions was between *transactional* and *transformational* leadership.[20] Transactional leadership is an exchange of something that has value both for leaders and for followers.[21] Transformational leadership is a process leaders and followers engage in that raises one another's level of morality and motivation by appealing to ideals and values.[22]

Leadership theory

John Dugan and Susan Komives write, "A historical examination of leadership theory reveals movement from models predicated on individual achievement, management, and positional authority to those associated with a concern for the common good, process orientations, and shared responsibility."[23]

Dugan and Komives continue: "Leader *selection* theories evolved to leader *training* and subsequently lead*er* development transitioned to leader*ship* development. This movement is often characterized as differentiating between two distinct theoretical paradigms: the industrial and the postindustrial."[24]

Industrial theory

- Individual achievement
- Management
- Positional authority
- Leader-centric
- Productivity focused

Theories within the industrial or conventional paradigm include trait-based, behavioral, situational, and expectancy-based theories.[25] These theories are often leader-centric with a strong emphasis on productivity, which focus entirely on individual skill development designed to increase positional role effectiveness or those that stress goal attainment over mutual development in the leadership process.[26]

The Adventist Church leadership evolved out of the industrial era, so we often behave this way. I heard a church leader say the Adventist Church is hierarchical; it's leader-centric and top-down. But the Bible says, "But many that are first shall be last; and the last shall be first" (Matthew 19:30, KJV). It should not be hierarchical, but a flat circle organization. There's a place for the church, conference, union, division, and general conference, and the head of the organization is Jesus. Everyone else is the arms, hands, fingers, toes, feet. We have different functions, roles, and responsibilities.

A church should not be a hierarchical infrastructure; but we came out of the industrial era and adopted industrial leadership, where the church behaves hierarchically. In fact, the industrial leadership focus is on transactional leadership. Transactional leadership is an exchange of something that has value both for leaders and for followers.[27] That's why church leaders are voted every one, or two, years—we transition people; yet, we don't do well coaching, mentoring, and nurturing people to become leaders. Sometimes, because of the limited time, we only want to train people to become me-chanics to work within the church industry. This is transactional leadership.

The ecclesiastical body of the church has adopted this industrial leadership hierarchical and departmental model, and challenged its effectiveness and efficiency. As the industrial age sustains its development using hierarchical, bureaucratic organizational structure, its structure is functional and each entity's role and responsibilities are clearly defined. In fact, when you read Exodus 18, I believe that God gives the concept of its structure to men through Moses' father-in-law, Jethro. So the structure itself is not the challenge, but people within the infrastructure. Members of industrial organizations can become territorial, departmentalize their specific roles and responsibilities, and create compartmentalized functions within its infrastructure: "My program, my ministry." We develop a compartmentalized cultural environment and end up creating organizational silos, organizational fragmentation, and a displacement culture within the church body.

Because of the displacement culture that we have created through the organizational silos, we don't collaborate with one another internally and externally. To some degree, the local church ministry departments are not collaborating with one another. The Adventist health-care and educational institutions and the ecclesiastical body of the church do not work collaboratively. It seems that each ministry department is working on its own projects, separate from others as independent organizations.

For example, a church recently voted in new church-board members and departmental leaders. The pastor told them at the first meeting, "For the next church board meeting, I want everyone to come back with your ministry ideas, plans, and budgets." So at the following meeting, the directors came together with the anticipation of presenting their yearly plans. The women's ministry director presented a plan for the second week of May. But, the children's ministry director said, "Wait, we want to do something that same week." Then the personal ministry director said, "I need one thousand dollars for a community outreach project." Then the other departments questioned in protest, "How could you ask for more, when we all get five hundred dollars per ministry?" And they basically argued for their own plans and piece of the financial pie.

This is an example of a church merely cooperating, not collaborating. Women's ministry rarely mixes with children's ministry. The men's ministry doesn't plan with youth ministry. Adventist Community Services doesn't get involved with prison ministry or the Adventist Development and Relief Agency. We compartmentalize, working in silos. We coexist and cooperate, and we wonder why our church isn't effective.

In the ideal world, what the board should have done was to spend two to three days planning together. They should have asked, "What are our core values? What is our vision? What is our mission? Why do we exist? How can we collaborate and support one another's dreams instead of working in our own silos?"

Utilizing the technique of group processes does not minimize an individual's strengths; instead, it enhances an individual's capacity. Through group processes, leaders share decision-making opportunities, which nurture group support of an action because one individual did not make the decision. It is extremely important to develop learning strategies for the group.

C. K. Prahalad indicates that "it is not enough just to have a strategic architecture [big picture]. A strategic architecture provides the company with a direction, but it needs to have the emotional and the intellectual energy to make the journey. It needs shared aspiration which allows the company to stretch itself beyond its current resources—one that provides a sense of direction, a sense of common purpose, a sense of destiny, a single-minded and inspiring challenge which commands the respect and the allegiance of every person in the organization."[28]

But because we utilize the industrial leadership model and the transactional leadership theory-based departmental function, we transact the leader every one or two years. It is my conviction that one of the first and foremost essential functions of the church is to equip and develop disciples who will make more disciples. However, the current church ministry infrastructure is not set up to support and enhance either leadership development or discipleship development. Leadership development and discipleship development requires a long-term commitment. It requires time and resources to increase leaders' knowledge, enhance their skills and competencies, and influence their attitude. However, in this short-term, limited period of transactional leadership environment, we don't develop confident leaders to become difference-makers and change agents—disciples.

We should transition from the industrial leadership to the postindustrial leadership theory and relationship-building model to engage in leadership and discipleship development.

Postindustrial leadership model
Today, we're living in the postindustrial, postmodern, post-Christian era. Leadership is not based on transaction, but transformation. We need

to nurture people to work together for the next three to five years as a team. No more departmental programs. We need to come together in core values where we work, corporately and collectively.

The postindustrial and relational theory or emergent paradigm includes leadership theories clustered around the themes of transformational influence, reciprocal relationships, complexity, and authenticity.[29] Dugan and Komives write, "These theories are often focused on the mutual development of leaders and followers in collaborative processes aimed at change for the common good. The shift to these new ways of conceptualizing leadership is attributed largely to James MacGregor Burns (1978) and his seminal work *Leadership*, which argued that leadership at its core was a value-based process that had to be focused on both leader and follower development. Burns's work paved the way for subsequent theorists who acknowledged the incredible complexity of leadership and increasingly emphasized perspectives associated with ethics and social justice."[30]

The transformational theory is a multidirectional relationship-building model in which anyone can be a leader and/or a follower; followers persuade leaders and other followers, leaders and followers may change places, and there are many different relationships that make up the overall relationship that is leadership, such as groups, departments, organizations, and so on.[31]

In addition, the transformation theory is based on noncoercive relationship, which is not based on authority, power, or dictatorial actions but is based on persuasive behaviors, allowing anyone in the relationship to freely agree or disagree and ultimately to drop into or out of the relationship.[32]

The industrial leadership theory based on transactional leadership development is a concept developed by *uniformity of command* in purpose under one responsible commander; the postindustrial leadership theory based on transformational leadership development is developed by *unity of efforts* in value among all leaders and followers.

Uniformity of command is one-size-fits-all. When I came to America, I heard, "America is a melting pot." I don't believe it's a melting pot, which implies one culture dominating the rest of society. But I like the thought of America as a taco salad or haystack—where there are different ingredients that create the tasty dish, all based on respect. We need to recognize the differences and attributes that contribute to the body of the organization. We will have greater unity in the organization because we're driven by values rather than by uniformity. We need to become a *unity of effort*, where we coordinate, cooperate, and collaborate with one another.

Entities must define core values of each organization and encourage all members to collaborate in their efforts to maximize the potential growth and impact in society.

What are we known for? What is our passion? What are our competencies and resources—both tangible and intangible? Why do we exist? This is why Jesus said, "Go and make disciples"—to equip, develop, educate, and enlighten people to become the change agents and difference-makers who will make more disciples. It is a personal development experience. Kegan and Lahey say, "Research shows that the single biggest cause of work burnout is not work overload, but working too long without experiencing your own personal development."[33]

The church must encourage leadership development and discipleship development, understand it as the most important function and purpose of the church, and develop and create a personal growth environment at all aspects of our engagements.

Equipping and developing disciples, knowledge workers, human resources is an integral part of church leadership that requires cultivating potential individuals and motivating them for the missional church movement. Also, investing in professional development and continual assessment of the person is an essential process of personal and professional growth.

Both Robert Kegan and William Torbert present that for successful organization growth, three stages of leadership development mind-sets are required: (1) socialized mind, (2) self-authoring mind, and (3) self-transforming mind.[34]

- *The social mind* is where the leaders develop team players, faithful followers, aligning with people, seeking direction, and building relationships.
- *The self-authoring mind* is where the leaders focus on an agenda, learn to lead, develop their own compass, develop their own frame of work, focus on problem-solving, and are independent.
- *The self-transforming mind* is where leaders become "meta-leaders," leaders of leaders who mobilize people and organizations to collaborate in times of crisis. A leader who leads to learn, developing multiple frames of work, and instead of problem-solving they are investing their time in problem-finding. It takes eight to ten years of journey to grow leadership.

But, if we are continually transitioning the church leaders every one or two years, not only will personal development opportunities cease to exist, but the organization will either maintain the status quo or begin to decline and lose its influence and impact in that community. We must invest our time and resources to educate and develop leaders who will become disciples through a long-term commitment to personal relationship development.

To begin, the local church should identify the core values of its ministry. *Why do we exist? What are our passions?* Then the church can build ministries/departments based on relevant values, to create a collaborative structured working environment. When we share the resources and workers across departments within the church, we create synergy in ministry and function in a unified way.

When you look at Acts 2, you'll see five core values:

1. Evangelism (vv. 41, 47)
2. Discipleship (v. 42)
3. Fellowship (vv. 42, 44–46)
4. Worship (vv. 42, 43, 46, 47)
5. Service (v. 43)

Actually, I believe everything they did was evangelistic. They shared the good news and demonstrated the love of God through worship, discipleship, fellowship, and community services. Whether we are young or old, male or female, it doesn't make a difference. Anyone who is interested in discipleship must come and work together. Because discipleship is a journey with Christ, it's a process. This is a mentoring and coaching process—to support each other to become faithful and committed disciples, to proclaim the good news, and to demonstrate the love of God.

Kegan and Lahey write about the Follower-Leader Organization (FLO) model:

> FLO involves four key roles: captain, coach, right hand, and left hand. Heading up a culture initiative is the role of the *captain*. At the heart of FLO's design is the role of the *coach*, which is filled by the person who most recently captained the same initiative. Her job, above all else, is to coach the captain in leadership and provide feedback that will help the captain develop his backhand.
>
> The *right hand* is the team member who works closely with the captain, knowing that she will someday soon take over as the next

captain as the roles rotate. Finally, the *left hand* is another team member who can contribute to the success of the initiative and is next in line to succeed the right hand.[35]

Let me apply this to the church—the roles will stay together as a team for the next five years and learn about the ministry, enhance it together, and mentor and coach one another to grow and mature their spirituality in Christ.

In addition, each group must develop a group learning culture. The culture should include the three most important characteristics of group dynamics: accountability, commitment, and trust (ACT).[36] When the group process is experienced in ACT, the result will be marvelous. The group will grow effectively and will operate as a team and through learning strategies build connections between each person.

When we change the local church leadership every one or two years, we are not being effective in developing disciples. In fact, this transactional leadership behavior is not based on the biblical model of discipleship. We need to learn to incorporate the transformational leadership theories through the FLO model to equip and develop faithful disciples—the difference-makers.

To invest in a ministry also means to invest in people and to develop individuals into more effective leaders—this will ensure the success of the ministry. Even if the ministry suffers, the demands in its sustainability and the investment in leaders will challenge them to initiate and implement new ministries wherever volunteers are located.

Discipleship is leadership development, and it takes time, but we want immediate gratification. That's why we love drive-through fast food, a drive-through at banks, and even drive-through church. Because of our immediate gratification culture, we've become Seventh-day *Event*ists, doing events instead of developing long-term sustainable community development outreach ministries. We have to change this *event*ist mentality and culture. Each church must define the core values of its entity and restructure the ministry based on the core values. We're not living in the analog age, but the digital age. We don't write letters anymore, but text. But our church ministry is still in the analog age, and the structure of our church ministry is still based on the industrial model. We must change this way of thinking and working so we can exist as a missional church in the present.

Arnon Reichers, John Wanous, and James Austin emphasize professional development in four specific ways by expanding practice opportunities, enhancing core capabilities, broadening perspectives, and learning collaborative leadership.[37] These four ways of human resource development indicate that it requires much time and resources to invest in people with long-term commitment.

Throughout my life, many individuals have inspired me in various situations, using opportunities to mentor intentionally and unintentionally. It is through social interaction that the connection between individuals to mentor or be mentored is brought about.

This is why Rost defines leadership as a no-supervisory relationship, which reflects the idea that leadership is based on complex interactions.[38] Leadership is a dynamic social and political relationship, based on a mutual development of purposes that may never be realized.

Jesus mentored disciples to become change agents, to influence the world. Behavioral change is the core of the matter when mentoring. Behavioral change happens in situations, mostly by interacting honestly and speaking to people's hearts. Mentoring is not about giving people an analysis of their behavior; it is about helping them to see the truth.

In order for individual and community development to succeed, we must provide relevant services through our community outreach ministries. Some non-Christians resent that churches don't pay taxes because the church is a nonprofit organization and occupies precious real estate in the community, but we provide no return for that occupation. The community sees no benefit from the irrelevant services.

A community outreach ministry in the missional church means more than a departmental engagement, such as Adventist Community Services or the Adventist Development and Relief Agency or other trained professionals. It is *every* Adventist being involved in the community outreach ministries and providing relevant services.

Because of lack of education or field-based experience, we face several significant challenges, such as these:

1. Pastoral understanding: Adventist pastors have a limited understanding of the full scope of community outreach ministry, leadership, managerial knowledge, and skills based upon evidence-based practices.
2. Need for mentoring resources: Mentoring opportunities are few. David Garvin indicated that this is a component particularly valuable to the utilization of innate qualities and knowledge, coupled with the need to learn skills crucial to leadership of successful

organizations in today's competitive and complex society.[39]

3. Lack of philanthropic orientation: While a giving mentality exists among constituents, a philanthropic orientation is not fully developed. Barry Dym and Harry Hutson emphasize that philanthropic traditions and their influences on financially healthy nonprofit institutions are needed.[40] Placing this critical component into a program of equipping and educating Adventist leaders and in the organizational context has been proven to strengthen and improve institutions. There is ample evidence among Adventist institutions that the lack of financial sustainability is a serious problem and has led to the demise of a significant number of institutions.

4. A lack of clearly defined mission: While developing quality professional leaders is a high priority, developing and maintaining spiritually strong leaders who personally possess and are able to cultivate distinctly Adventist mission-oriented values in the faculty, staff, and students is the highest priority for the church. To this end, a program should include experiences and seminars to help participants to strengthen their relationship with God and to refine ways to infuse the system with those values.

The evolution of the leadership theories reflects a complex movement from a hierarchical leadership-centric model to a team-centric management model, orientated in engaging individuals toward group goals and achievement.[41] Most of these theories are characterized by social responsibility, developmental concern, and process orientations. The body of literature on leadership theory stems largely from these latter theories and offers a rich source for grounding leadership development programs.

Relational leadership model
Susan Komives developed the relational leadership model. The model builds upon postindustrial models of leadership, emphasizing reciprocal relationships. The theoretical model defines leadership as a relational and ethical process of people attempting together to accomplish positive change.[42] The model is comprised of five key components: purposefulness, inclusiveness, empowerment, ethical practices, and a process orientation. It is among the few models that explicitly include ethics as a necessary and inherent dimension to leadership. The model supports individuals to expand their capacity to be effective in engaging with others in a leadership context or setting.

Relationships were vital to Jesus' leadership style. If we apply His principles today, leadership will be focused on relationships. Influencing people's behavior will be important, but understanding a person's problems and circumstances will be the foundation of leading. The leader will have a keen ability to analyze a situation and recognize diverse points of view. The leader will be known as a change agent and valuable mentor. We see Jesus' example in the way that He led His disciples. Jesus was in tune with others. He felt their pain. He knew their loss. He was affected by how others felt, and He responded to them with love and compassion.

Whether it's leadership definition or organizational structure, it's clear that we should continually seek the true meaning of leadership—leading servants. As God came to serve, we ought also to follow in His footsteps and let our lives influence the lives of others. Then constituents will follow, not because they have to, but because they want to.

> "People don't care how much you know until they know how much you care."
> —Zig Ziglar

Zig Ziglar said, "People don't care how much you know until they know how much you care."[43] Leadership is to lead by integrity and influence, and my prayer is that we will equip and develop ourselves to become more effective servant leaders for our God and His ministry. Leadership is an influence. It is relational, not coercive. Leadership exists in multidirectional structure, not just top-down hierarchy structure. It is based on the competencies of each individual, regardless of their status or position. Leadership is not solely based on authority or power, but on trusted relationships. It happens in a safe environment where everyone is appreciated and heard.

Organizations should invest in equipping and developing leadership with long-term commitment.[44] Enhancement of individual leadership capacity is essential, especially creating an environment where individuals work with other team members to contribute individual capabilities to the achievement of group objectives and work effectively with others in a group setting. The church leadership should not be hierarchical; its organizational structure should be flat.

Since God is the head of the organization and there are many parts of the body, all are important. We have to learn to collaborate with each unit of the organization. In order for individual and community development to succeed, it is necessary to guide people's behavior. Leadership requires leaders to improve their skills, not so much their technical skills that develop methodology, but to focus on educational and structural aspects of understanding a person's problems and circumstances.[45] The ability to support and analyze a situation and recognize the diversified points of view is one of the most important leadership characteristics of change agents and coaches.

Leaders influence not only through their performance but also through their characters. People must be connected, instead of just being coworkers.[46] All the people in the organization should exercise leadership, and their leadership skills should be developed. Every person should be a leader and a follower. One should know when and where each role must be demonstrated. All of us want to become a leader and not a follower, but in biblical concepts, we should be leading servants, as our Lord came to serve, not to be served.

Leaders should utilize the following managerial perspectives to enhance organizational behavior: facilitative, collaborative, and directive:[47]

Nature of participative leadership[48]

- Facilitative/Delegation: $A = B, C$
- Collaborative/Joint Decision: $A = AB, AC$
- Directive/Autocratic Decision: $A = A$

1. **Facilitative/Delegation:** This type of leadership is critical to good team function. You may have an agenda, but if the group presents a better alternative, you adopt their recommendation. This is key to being a motivator and to encouraging others to lead. For example, this is where a leader participates in a meeting with an A agenda, but you come out of the meeting with a B solution. Facilitative leaders make things easier and help get things done. A facilitative leader recognizes the synergy of bringing together the different strengths of individuals. It has been said, "You can do what I cannot do. I can do what you cannot do. Together we can do great things."[49] A facilitative leader should make everyone feel involved and engaged. Team members should be willing to brainstorm and generate lots of ideas. Meetings should result in purpose, directions, and actions agreed upon by everyone.
   Specific skills of a facilitative leader include:
   - Building rapport—establishing credibility to enable people to contribute with ease
   - Communicating effectively verbally and nonverbally— being supportive and engaged

- Listening actively—demonstrating your interest by your body language

2. **Collaborative/Joint Decision:** Collaborative leadership promotes working together to look for ways to merge ideas. This strengthens working relationships and develops a sense of accomplishment and oneness. For example, a leader participates in a meeting with an *A* agenda but comes out of the meeting with an *AB* solution. Collaborative leaders intentionally manage relationships so that others can succeed while accomplishing a collective goal. They help two or more people in a group to work toward a shared outcome in a collective, respectful way. The ability to sustain positive relationships is critical to collective leadership.

   Specific skills of a collective leader include the following:
   - Listening without judging
   - Knowing your team
   - Disagreeing politely
   - Encouraging participation
   - Making sure everyone has a turn
   - Providing a safe environment for discussion
   - Acknowledging people's points of view, feelings, and input
   - Elaborating without giving answers
   - Asking questions
   - Checking for understanding
   - Providing critique without attacking the person
   - Summarizing ideas
   - Clarifying the goal and keeping everyone on track

3. **Directive/Autocratic Decision:** Directive leadership involves dictating and instructing. This may be necessary if the group does not see the big picture in the same way you do. You will have to lead the team members with charisma, challenging them beyond their imagination. For example, a leader participates in a meeting with an *A* agenda and comes out of the meeting with an *A* solution. Directive leadership requires management skills to deal with the practical aspects of any organization. There are many times when directive leadership is necessary in order to get things done. Directive leaders accomplish goals by giving clear directions, establishing goals and objectives, setting evaluation criteria and timelines, and designating roles and responsibilities. Being direc-

tive ensures accuracy and eliminates time-consuming mistakes. This type of leadership can be seen as autocratic. The leader focuses his or her interactions with followers on goal accomplishment and achievement and spends a small amount of time using supportive behaviors described in the other two types of leadership. Directive leaders need to take care not to abuse their power. This type of leadership is effective when followers are inexperienced, new employees, or volunteers, or there is a tight time frame for accomplishing a goal. It is a leadership style that accommodates diverse people from many different generations or maturity levels. Followers have an increased sense of security and control.

Specific skills of directive leadership (management) include:
• Giving directions
• Guiding and structuring the activities of the followers
• Planning and scheduling
• Assigning responsibilities
• Defining roles and communication patterns of the followers
• Motivating and conveying expertise
• Monitoring and following up on assignment completion
• Determining expectations, goals, and work methods

Now, which is the most effective leadership style or technique? Honestly, it's all three of them. As a leader you need to recognize when to use each style of leadership.

Imagine I am the pilot of a plane, and you are my passenger. I have a copilot, and we're at the nearest airport of wherever you are. From this airport, we go to Seoul, South Korea—Incheon Airport. The plane is on the runway, and I'm about to take off. Right now, the copilot is not involved in this process. I am the pilot in charge and no one is involved. I am directive and autocratic.

Once we're in the air, I transition from manual to autopilot. My copilot and I are now collaborating and making decisions together; I'm involving others. I am removing myself from direct control, and I'm being collaborative.

After the airplane has completely transitioned into autopilot, I can take a break and walk to the galley, review the flight schedule with the flight attendants, eat my meal—I am not in charge; my copilot is in charge. I'm currently facilitating.

At last, I'm back in my seat, and I see the Inchoen Airport (the best international airport for more than a decade; something you just needed to know). I renegotiate with my copilot and I take the responsibility from him or her. I'm being collaborative, again. Now, I'm landing the plane and no one is involved in this moment. I am the pilot and I am in charge; I'm directive again.

Now, who is the most effective leader? The answer is all of them. You need to know when to be directive, when to be collaborative, when to be facilitating. When you're directive all the time, they call you a dictator. When you're facilitating all the time, they call you a wimp, because you're not taking any risk. You can't be just one type for too long—this is a situational leadership: knowing when to be directive and knowing when to facilitate. The most difficult thing in life is changing people's minds. But when you influence others because your heart is connected to their heart, then awesome things happen.

In addition, there are categories of taxonomy of leadership skills that leaders should understand and develop—technical, interpersonal, and conceptual skills:[50]

1. Technical skills—As a knowledge worker and technologist, a leader should know all technical aspects of the responsibility.
2. Interpersonal skills—Leading an organization is about leading people. People skills is a crucial component of success in organizational growth. Understand how and why people behave in certain ways.
3. Conceptual skills—Leaders should consistently apply didactic learning processes into leadership. Theory and real-life experience must accompany the analytical ability of leadership. Comprehend circumstances and working environments, and continually enhance and improve them for the employees.

Technical skills: Know the methods, processes, procedures, and techniques for conducting a specialized activity, and the ability to use tools and equipment relevant to that activity. Technical skills are primarily the ability to accomplish tasks, utilize personnel and resources effectively, and maintain order and reliable processes of operation. The leader should know as much about the technical aspects of their responsibilities as possible. Perhaps the most important aspects of the technical leadership skills are making decisions and managing information. A good knowledge base about all the aspects of your organization is necessary in order to assess each situation and help guide your team to the best outcomes.

Interpersonal skills: Recognize human behavior and interpersonal processes; be able to understand the feelings, attitudes, and motives of others from what they say and do. Communicate clearly and effectively and establish effective and cooperative relationships. Interpersonal skills are the ability to develop positive relationships. It's about leading people. This includes improving relationships between yourself as the leader and those you work with, and facilitating relationships between your volunteers. The focus should be to increase cooperation and teamwork, and build organizational identity and pride. Relationship skills are critical to the success in organizational growth. It is important that a leader understand how and why people behave the way they do, and then implement positive motivational methods to guide them in the mission.

Conceptual skills: These involve the general analytical ability to think logically, formulate concepts, and make the connection between ideas and concepts. Leaders should consistently think of themselves as teaching leaders, which of course means that they are also learning leaders. This includes the ability to generate creative ideas and generate solutions for problems. In addition, conceptual leadership includes the ability to analyze programs, predict problems or changes that may be necessary, and recognize opportunities.

In the beginning of your ministry, you have to demonstrate your *technical skill set*. People need to know you have what it takes to lead your ministry. That's why having a transitional leadership every year isn't favorable, because it takes times to develop a skill set. As you grow within that structure, whether in three or five years, you need to invest more time in a *conceptual skill set*. Not just doing the job, but figuring out how to enhance the ministry, the journey. Think about how to invest your time and resources; figure where you are in the organization's growth.

Leadership team development

Through this journey, we develop a leadership team, which is a critical component that must be implemented effectively for the long-term missional church movement. After all, Jesus developed a team to carry out His ministry. It's not a one-man show. But oftentimes, there are too many "lonely rangers" in the church, saying, "I've been doing this for so many years, and that's the way it goes."

Glenn Parker suggests that there are four types of team members we need to develop:[51]

Contributor—task oriented

Positive	Negative
Enjoys providing the team with good technical information and data	Pushes for unrealistic performance standards
Does their homework	Loses sight of the big picture
Pushes the team to set high performance standards	Lacks patience with team climate and process issues
Uses resources wisely	Becomes impatient with other team members who do not live up to the contributor's standards
Can be depended on to do what is asked of them	

Everyone has strengths and weaknesses. But contributors are task-oriented people. They are dependable, systematic, proficient, and efficient. If you need someone to do something over the weekend, you ask a contributor. They will sacrifice their family time to get the job done. They see the trees they need to chop down. But they are also shortsighted, data bound, perfectionistic, and narrow-visioned. They see the trees but they don't see the forest.

Collaborator—goal oriented

Positive	Negative
Helps the team establish goals, objectives, and action plans	Does not give attention to the basic team tasks
Pitches in to help out other members who need help	Fails to periodically revisit or challenge the mission or goals
Is willing to work outside their defined role to help the team	Does not focus on the individual needs of team members
Works hard to achieve team goals even if they don't agree with them	Complains about lack of progress toward team goals
	Does not give sufficient attention to the process by which goals are reached

Collaborators are goal-oriented people. They are forward-looking people—they have a vision. They are thinking five years down the line and are imaginative. Because they are so futuristic, they are not realistic—they see the forest but they don't know which trees to chop down. That's why you need both contributors and collaborators.

Communicator—process oriented

Positive	Negative
Helps the team relax and have fun by joking, laughing, and discussing personal interests	Sees team process and climate as an end in itself
Steps in to resolve process problems	Fails to challenge or contradict other team members
Listens attentively to all viewpoints	Does not recognize the importance of task accomplishment
Recognizes and praises other team members for their efforts	Overuses humor and other process techniques

Communicators are process-oriented people. They encourage; they see the five-year plan; they carefully monitor and evaluate every year, making changes to meet the goal; they remind the rest of the team to be faithful to the end. But they are so polite they are not practical. They are nonconfrontational, not wanting to offend—they are postmodern, feeling-based people.

Challenger—question oriented

Positive	Negative
Willing to disagree with the team leader	Does not know when to back off
Candidly shares their views about the work of the team	Pushes the team to unreasonable risks
Challenges the team to take well-considered risks	Becomes rigid and inflexible
Pushes the team to set high ethical standards for their work	Paints themselves into a corner
Willing to back off when their views are not accepted	Too direct in communicating with other team members

Challengers are very candid, honest, principle-oriented, and assertive people. But they are also rigid, arrogant, self-righteous, aggressive, questioning, and critical.

We need to have all four types of people to work collectively—this will be a healthy environment. You may want everyone to be like you, to behave like you, to think like you, but that's unhealthy and boring, surrounded by yes-people. You need to have all four attributes to have a vibrant organization. Diversity equals creativity. If we don't value diversity, we won't be innovative.

What happens when you don't have all four types of members? You, as the leader, play the role that the team needs until you find a new member who can fill the role. You need to challenge, to communicate, or collaborate, and recognize these types in your members and support their different personalities.

No more using friends that you like to work with, or family members who do what you say. You need to be challenged; your thought process has to be stretched and taught to see beyond the usual scenario.

Team building requires the leader to notice what the team is accomplishing and say something about it. One of the easiest ways to motivate others is to appropriately affirm your team members. According to Phyllis Theroux, "One of the commodities in life that most people can't get enough of is compliments. The ego is never so intact that one can't find a hole in which to plug a little praise. But, compliments by their very nature are highly biodegradable and tend to dissolve hours or days after we receive them—which is why we can always use another."[52]

Know the people you work with; get to know your team members. Spend time outside the church; go camping together or have fellowship at someone's home. At church, we come together for a few hours, and then go home. And we wonder why we fight over minor issues.

Here's an example of what not to do: we appoint someone to a job, because of a specific talent or skill set. Then we dump a whole different set of responsibilities that has nothing to do with that person's skill set. Soon, we focus on that person's ineffectiveness or failures and complain about how that person is wasting time or not doing something well. That person eventually becomes discouraged and burned out. Once that person feels unappreciated and criticized, the person eventually leaves the toxic environment. Affirmation is free. Make sure you use it generously.

Let us become leading servants to serve God and His people!

In conclusion

Through the PhD program in leadership at Andrews University, I had the opportunity to review two important studies: epistemology[53] and anthropology.[54] Epistemology, the study of knowledge, asks, *How do we know what we know?* Anthropology, the study of sources and beginnings, asks, *Where did we come from?* These two studies have led me to explore four important questions in our lives: *Who am I? Where did I come from? What is my destiny? Which question is most important?* And it seems that we cannot answer *Who am I?* or *What is my destiny?* unless we first answer, *Where did I come from?*—which is the source of reason and existence. In my conviction, the key question is the second one: *Where did I come from?* Depending on your answer, your destiny will be changed.

Anatole France says, "The average man does not know what to do with this life, yet wants another one which will last forever."[55] When was the last time that you thought, *How do I turn myself into a missionary? How do I deploy myself as a missionary in a community transformation?* Since we are called into the servanthood of Christianity, we ought to take the gospel to the marketplace. Jesus went to the places where the people were. Likewise, we need churches where people are—at the mall, supermarkets, and coffee shops. For the most part, people are not coming to us; we have to go to them. Being a servant requires that we continually adopt new ways of thinking and working.

As leading servants, are we making any impact on the communities in which our institutions are located? *What about our churches, schools, and hospitals? Are they better places to live because of our existence in these communities?* The challenge is *not* about our ability to do this; it is about our *pride* and *our lack of concern for people.* That is what God is concerned about. We must pray for God's intervention in our lives and listen to people's struggles and challenges, looking for an opportunity to serve and demonstrate the love of God.

Since becoming a Christian, the purpose of my life is clearly defined. Simply, I am a child of God, who was created by His will, and my destiny is to be with Him eternally. My life was uncertain before I accepted Jesus Christ as my Lord and Savior, but a deep sense of assurance in His guidance leads me to trust in His Word. As a converted Christian, I've established a new set of values and principles for my life that continually motivate me to serve, even though there are a number of external influencing factors that discourage my steadfast love of God and Christian values. It is my sincere desire to become a faithful leading servant for my Lord, to share the good news, and to make a difference of eternal significance for others in our community.

If we say there is no God, only two things matter to us in this life—"to maximize our pleasure and minimize our pain." This means we don't have to care about people who are naked, sick, behind prison bars, or dying of hunger. Our only concern is that our wants and self-gratifications are fulfilled. But for those who believe there is a God, they have, or should have, a different perspective on life. Their attitude toward people is to put others before themselves and to be equally concerned about others as they are about themselves. This is what it means to be a Christian—to share your life with others as Christ shared His life for us. This is why I am a Christian who belongs to God—the Creator, Redeemer, and merciful and graceful Judge—and I am willing to be His instrument to serve others.

Ayn Rand said, "Throughout the centuries there were men who took first steps down new roads armed with nothing but their own vision."[56] I have to envision the innovative direction most appropriate for the operation and motivate our people to catch the vision, to become better equipped, and to challenge them to stay on the cutting edge. In most cases, to lead the church ministries in a new direction, I have to take the "first steps down new roads."

As our Lord and Christ had a dream to change the world for the kingdom of God, my desire is to be a change agent for Him. I consider being invited to be a part of God's mission and His dream a privilege and an awesome honor. I pray that you will also answer His call.

Let's build the kingdom of God, the kingdom of grace, in our families, neighborhoods, communities, societies, and on the earth!

1. Joseph C. Rost, *Leadership for the Twenty-First Century* (Westport, CT: Praeger, 1993).

2. Karen Seashore Louis et al., "Learning From Leadership: Investigating the Links to Improved Student Learning" (report, University of Minnesota / University of Toronto / Wallace Foundation, July 2010), 42, 50.

3. Susan R. Komives, "Advancing Leadership Education," in *The Handbook for Student Leadership Development*, 2nd edition, ed. Susan R. Komives et al. (San Francisco: Jossey-Bass, 2011), 6.

4. Komives, "Advancing Leadership Education," 6; James MacGregor Burns, *Leadership* (New York: Harper & Row, 1978).

5. Komives, "Advancing Leadership Education," 6; Michael Harvey and Ronald E. Riggio, eds., *Leadership Studies: The Dialogue of Disciplines*, New Horizons in Leadership Studies (Cheltenham, UK: Edward Elgar, 2011).

6. Komives, "Advancing Leadership Education," 6; Donald M. Wolfe and David A. Kolb, "Career Development, Personal Growth, and Experiential Learning," in *Organizational Psychology: Readings on Human Behavior in Organizations*, 4th edition, ed. David A. Kolb,

Irwin M. Rubin, and James M. McIntyre (Englewood Cliffs, NJ: Prentice-Hall, 1984).

7. Alice Y. Kolb, and David A. Kolb, "Experiential Learning Theory," in *Encyclopedia of the Sciences of Learning*, ed. Norbert M. Seel (New York: Springer, 2012), 1215–1219.

8. Marcia B. Baxter Magolda, "Epistemological Reflection: The Evolution of Epistemological Assumptions From Age 18 to 30," in *Personal Epistemology: The Psychology of Beliefs About Knowledge and Knowing*, ed. Barbara K. Hofer and Paul R. Pintrich (Mahwah, NJ: Lawrence Erlbaum Associates, 2002), 89–102.

9. John P. Dugan and Susan R. Komives, "Leadership Theories," in Komives et al., *Handbook for Student Leadership Development*, 43, 44; Komives, "Advancing Leadership Education," 6; James Kouzes and Barry Posner, *The Leadership Challenge: How to Make Extraordinary Things Happen in Organizations*, 5th ed. (San Francisco: Jossey-Bass, 2012).

10. Dugan and Komives, "Leadership Theories," 44; Barry Z. Posner, "A Longitudinal Study Examining Changes in Students' Leadership Behavior," *Journal of College Student Development* 50, no. 5 (September/October 2009): 551–563.

11. Dugan and Komives, "Leadership Theories," 44.

12. Dugan and Komives, "Leadership Theories," 44; Peter G. Northouse, *Leadership: Theory and Practice*, 6th ed. (Thousand Oaks, CA: SAGE Publications, 2013).

13. "Foundations of Leadership Education," in Komives et al., *Handbook for Student Leadership Development*, 33.

14. Dugan and Komives, "Leadership Theories," 35.

15. Dennis C. Roberts, *Student Leadership Programs in Higher Education* (ACPA Media, Southern Illinois University Press, 1981), 212.

16. Van Velsor and McCauley, "Our View of Leadership Development," 2.

17. Ibid., 18.

18. Ledbetter, Banks, and Greenhalgh, *Reviewing Leadership*, 109 (italics in the original).

19. White, *Acts of the Apostles*, 210.

20. Kelly M. Hannum, Jennifer W. Martineau, and Claire Reinelt, eds., *The Handbook of Leadership Development Evaluation* (San Francisco: Jossey-Bass, 2007), 5; James MacGregor Burns, "Transactional and Transforming Leadership," in *Leading Organizations: Perspectives for a New Era*, ed. Gill Robinson Hickman (Thousand Oaks, CA: SAGE Publications, 1998), 133, 134.

21. Hannum, Martineau, and Reinelt, *Handbook of Leadership Development Evaluation*, 5; K. W. Kuhnert and P. Lewis, "Transactional and Transformational Leadership: A Constructive/Developmental Analysis," *Academy of Management Review* 12, no. 4, (October 1, 1987): 648–657.

22. Hannum, Martineau, and Reinelt, *Handbook of Leadership Development Evaluation*, 5; Gary A. Yukl, *Leadership in Organizations*, 8th ed. (Upper Saddle River, NJ: Pearson, 2013).

23. Dugan and Komives, "Leadership Theories," 37; see also Northouse, *Leadership: Theory and Practice*.

24. Dugan and Komives, "Leadership Theories," 37 (italics in the original); see also Joseph C. Rost, "Leadership Development in the New Millennium," *Journal of Leadership & Organizational Studies* 1, no. 1 (November 1, 1993): 91–110.

25. Dugan and Komives, "Leadership Theories," 37; Northouse, *Leadership: Theory and Practice*.

26. Dugan and Komives, "Leadership Theories," 37; Susan R. Komives, Nance Lucas, and Timothy R. McMahon, *Exploring Leadership: For College Students Who Want to Make a Difference*, 2nd ed. (San Francisco: Jossey-Bass, 2007).

27. Hannum, Martineau, and Reinelt, *Handbook of Leadership Development Evaluation*, 5; J. M. Howell and B. J. Avolio, "Transformational Leadership, Transactional Leadership, Focus of Control, and Support for Innovation: Key Predictors of Consolidated-Business-Unit Performance," *Journal of Applied Psychology* 78, no. 6 (1993): 891.

28. C. K. Prahalad, "Strategies for Growth," in *Rethinking the Future*, ed. Rowan Gibson (London: Nicholas Brealey, 1998), 69; see also Gary Hamel and C. K. Prahalad, "Competing for the Future," *Futures: The Journal of Policy, Planning and Futures Studies* 28, no. 1 (February 1996): 91.

29. Dugan and Komives, "Leadership Theories," 40; Northouse, *Leadership: Theory and Practice*.

30. Dugan and Komives, "Leadership Theories," 40; see also Burns, "Transactional and Transforming Leadership," 133, 134.

31. Robert Hooijberg, "A Multidirectional Approach Toward Leadership: An Extension of the Concept of Behavioral Complexity," *Human Relations*, 49, no. 7 (July 1, 1996): 917–946.

32. Rost, *Leadership for the Twenty-First Century*, 107; Robert W. Rowden, "The Relationship Between Charismatic Leadership Behaviors and Organizational Commitment," *Leadership & Organization Development Journal* 21, no. 1 (2000): 30–35.

33. Kegan and Lahey, *An Everyone Culture*, introduction.

34. Robert Kegan, *In Over Our Heads* (Cambridge, MA: Harvard University Press, 1994); William R. Torbert, *Managing the Corporate Dream* (Homewood, IL: Dow Jones-Irwin, 1987).

35. Kegan and Lahey, *An Everyone Culture*, 22 (italics in the original).

36. Errol E. Joseph and Bruce E. Winston, "A Correlation of Servant Leadership, Leader Trust, and Organizational Trust," *Leadership & Organization Development Journal* 26, no. 1 (2005): 6–22.

37. Arnon E. Reichers, John P. Wanous, and James T. Austin, "Understanding and Managing Cynicism About Organizational Change," *Academy of Management Executive* 11, no. 1 (February 1997): 48–59.

38. Rost, *Leadership for the Twenty-First Century*.

39. David A. Garvin, *Learning in Action: A Guide to Putting the Learning Organization to Work* (Boston: Harvard Business School Press, 2000).

40. Barry Dym and Harry Hutson, *Leadership in Nonprofit Organizations* (Thousand Oaks, CA: SAGE Publications, 2005).

41. Kenneth Leithwood et al., "How Leadership Influences Student Learning (Review of Research)" (report, University of Minnesota / University of Toronto / Wallace Foundation, 2004).

42. John P. Dugan and Susan R. Komives, *Developing Leadership Capacity in College Students* (College Park, MD: National Clearinghouse for Leadership Programs, 2007).

43. Zig Ziglar, http://www.goodreads.com/quotes/863418-people-don-t-care-how-much-you-know-until-they-know.

44. Terry D. Anderson with Ron Ford and Marilyn Hamilton, *Transforming Leadership: Equipping Yourself and Coaching Others to Build the Leadership Organization*, 2nd ed. (Boca Raton, FL: CRC Press, 1998).

45. A. Lorri Mariasse, "Vision and Leadership: Paying Attention to Intention," *Peabody Journal of Education* 63, no. 1 (1985-1986): 150–173.

46. Jay A. Conger and Rabindra N. Kanungo, "Toward a Behavioral Theory of Charismatic Leadership in Organizational Settings," *Academy of Management Review* 12, no. 4 (October 1, 1987): 637–647.

47. Rodney T. Ogawa et al., "CHAT-IT: Toward Conceptualizing Learning in the Context of Formal Organizations," *Educational Researcher* 37, no. 2 (March 1, 2008): 83–95.

48. Frank A. Heller, "Leadership, Decision Making, and Contingency Theory," *Industrial Relations: A Journal of Economy and Society* 12, no. 2 (May 1973): 183–199.

49. Quote often attributed to Mother Teresa, but see http://www.motherteresa .org/08_info/Quotesf.html.

50. Yukl, *Leadership in Organizations*.

51. Glenn M. Parker, *Team Players and Teamwork* (San Francisco: Jossey-Bass, 1990).

52. Quoted at Hans Finzel, "Why People Crave Affirmation in the Workplace," September 12, 2014, http://www.hansfinzel.com/41-power-affirmation-leadership/.

53. Kai Hahlweg and C. A. Hooker, eds., *Issues in Evolutionary Epistemology* (Albany, NY: SUNY Press, 1989).

54. Victor W. Turner and Edward M. Bruner, *The Anthropology of Experience* (University of Illinois Press, 1986).

55. Anatole France, https://www.great-quotes.com/quote/122613.

56. Ayn Rand, https://www.goodreads.com/quotes/310800-throughout-the-centuries -there-were-men-who-took-first-steps.

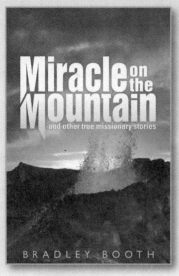

Miracle on the Mountain

Miracle on the Mountain is a collection of twelve extraordinary mission stories of faith and courage from around the globe. Stand alongside Li Hua and Segfred as they face certain death. Walk beside Genya and Won Tak as they preach the gospel against all odds, and journey with Philipp and Thomas to the ends of the earth to share the truth of the three angels' messages.
Perfect Bound, 128 Pages
ISBN 13: 978-0-8163-4106-1

Never Lose Hope

The story of a young Cuban pastor, separated from his pregnant wife, who is suddenly thrust behind bars because of his religious convictions. There, the faith he had cultivated as a child led him to facilitate in those cells the birth of an underground church.
Perfect Bound, 160 Pages
ISBN 13: 978-0-8163-6191-5

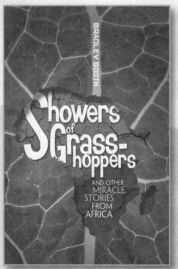

Showers of Grasshoppers

Showers of Grasshoppers and Other Miracle Stories From Africa chronicles the experiences of believers whose faithfulness in the little things prepared them to be faithful when times were the hardest, and the miracles God worked to save their lives.
Perfect Bound, 128 Pages
ISBN 13: 978-0-8280-2653-6

Pacific Press®
Publishing Association

"Where the Word Is Life"

Three ways to order:

1 Local	Adventist Book Center®
2 Call	1-800-765-6955
3 Shop	AdventistBookCenter.com

 AdventistBookCenter.com   AdventistBookCenter   @AdventistBooks   AdventistBooks

The Prodigal Daughter
by Kay D. Rizzo

The Prodigal Daughter is based on the true story of a young and gifted woman who leaves home amid the protests and tears of her father. Headstrong and determined to become a star, Brianna soon finds herself swept into a world far different from the life of fame and riches she'd expected. As her dreams begin to crumble, little does she realize the horror into which she is about to plunge. Like Jesus' story of another errant child, *The Prodigal Daughter* portrays a father's love and reminds us of how far our heavenly Father will go in order to redeem and restore His lost children.

Perfect Bound, 160 Pages
ISBN 13: 978-0-8163-5420-7

Backstage Pass
by Naomi Striemer

Eighteen-year-old Naomi stepped into one of the most prestigious board rooms known to musicians—Sony Records—and walked out a few minutes later with a record deal. Naomi was hailed by critics as "the next Celine Dion." But one conversation changed it all. *Backstage Pass* is the candid account of an up-and-coming recording artist who left everything to follow Christ.

Perfect Bound, 192 Pages
ISBN 13: 978-0-8163-4518-2

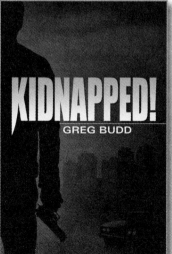

Kidnapped!
by Greg Budd

This is no ordinary story, and Paul Ratsara is no ordinary man. Raised in poverty and darkness, Paul Ratsara is a living example of the remarkable deliverance and transformation that a relationship with Christ brings. Every chapter radiates with confidence in a miracle-working God, who is bigger than our problems and greater than our difficulties.

Perfect Bound, 160 Pages
ISBN 13: 978-0-8163-4676-9

Pacific Press®
Publishing Association

"Where the Word Is Life"

Three ways to order:

1	Local	Adventist Book Center®
2	Call	1-800-765-6955
3	Shop	AdventistBookCenter.com

 AdventistBookCenter.com AdventistBookCenter @AdventistBooks 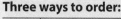 AdventistBooks

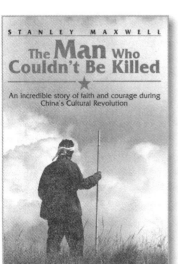